Towards Emotional

Literacy

Towards Emotional
Literacy

Susie Orbach

A *Virago* Book

Published by Virago Press 1999

Copyright © Susie Orbach 1999

Reprinted 2000

The moral right of the author has been asserted

A CIP catalogue record for this book
is available from the British Library

ISBN 1 86049 654 7

Typeset in Garamond by M Rules
Printed and bound in Great Britain by
Clays Ltd, St Ives plc

Virago Press
A Division of
Little, Brown and Company (UK)
Brettenham House
Lancaster Place
London WC2E 7EN

For
**Lukie, Lianna,
Joseph, Gudrun and Pat**

Acknowledgements

My *Guardian* column during the 1990s has been a way of having a conversation with a readership interested in the relationship between emotional issues and how they impact on public and private life. It has allowed me to explore the psychological relationship between the private and the public in broad brush strokes, as well as describe in considerable detail how we manage emotional responses inside ourselves. It has been a fantastically valuable way to develop my own ideas and I am very grateful to the readers for supporting the column and for their engagement with it. I am grateful to the various *Guardian* editors who over the years have found space for me: Deborah Orr, Helen Oldfield, Kath Viner, Roger Alton and Ian Katz.

Lennie Goodings, my lovely editor, once again chose the categories into which we could organise the pieces. During a frantic session, with literally scores of articles and typescripts arrayed over my desk, we sat together and selected the ones that would go in this collection and where we would put them. Lennie not only made logic out of a mass of material but also made the mechanics of doing so as enjoyable as such a task could be. Many thanks.

Andrea Collett shared with me the incredibly tedious job of going through my original typescripts and those of the *Guardian* to amend them. She was able to pick up when a crucial thought had been left out or distorted and then restore it to this manuscript. It was a very long job and she was thorough and thoughtful. Her equanimity was astounding. There is no way I could have done it without her. Thank you very much, Andrea.

Thank you too, to Jean Maund who copy-edited the manuscript, working off the small print of the newspaper articles. That can't have been easy.

As ever, Joseph Schwartz has been generous in reading and commenting on every piece when it was written. He has questioned, strengthened and many times helped me to clarify what I wanted to say and thus made it all possible. Thank you.

Contents

SECTION IV   Men, Women, Boys, Girls

SECTION V   Therapy

Introduction

The last five years have seen an unprecedented interest in emotional issues as they relate both to our private individual lives and to the public sphere. The idea of emotional literacy is one that is gaining currency. We no longer wonder what it can refer to, even if we find the concept difficult to define. The idea of emotional literacy has seeped into our consciousness – in whatever form – because it reflects a need we have to better understand the emotional dimensions of our lives.

Where truths evaporate or are superseded by other equally plausible truths, where ideologies and isms change before our eyes, where a (shared) moralism has collapsed, an unsettled uneasiness permeates our lives, encouraging us to find new ways of connecting and defining ourselves and the truths that we can live by. In the search to do so, we are increasingly regarding our personal experience and the emotional states that we inhabit as being of value.

Hesitantly we begin to question our rationalistic modes of thought. Are they as comprehensive as we have believed them to be? Is there a way in which our customary modes of thinking preclude or exclude experiences which are important? Could we expand what it is possible to think about? In what ways does our current thinking constrain us? Are there ways in which our thinking is built on a less rational basis than it claims? To what extent do our emotional lives affect what it is possible for us to countenance and hence think about?

Emotional literacy, in its simplest definition, means the capacity to register our emotional responses to the situations we are in and to acknowledge those responses to ourselves so that we recognise the ways in which they influence our thoughts and our actions. It is not about the elevation of emotional responses above all others, nor about the broadcasting of our emotions to those around us. Emotional literacy is the attempt to take responsibility for understanding our personal emotions.

It is a non-trivial undertaking. Emotions look like one thing on the surface and another at the depths. Just as letters and numbers need to be studied so that the jumbled symbols they start out as coalesce into forms which we can then decode and manipulate, so too do our emotions demand attention. The three Rs of registering, recognising and querying our immediate emotional responses allow us to note and reflect on our emotional reactions. At first we register that something has touched us in one way or another. We can then go on to name the emotional response. Thirdly, we can see whether what we feel constitutes the whole of what we are feeling, or whether more complex emotional responses are embedded within it.

As many of the pieces in this collection aim to show, emotions may be more complicated than they appear on the surface. What seems at first glance to be anger may turn out to hide a more subtle feeling that we may have less confidence in describing, such as disappointment. What appears to be righteous indignation may conceal troubling feelings involving a lack of self-worth. Unpleasant or even violent feelings aroused in us by others may turn out to be the projection of personal feelings which we don't know how to accept in ourselves. In applying the three Rs of emotional literacy we enhance our understanding. We are in a position to rein back aspects of ourselves which we have foisted on others. And we are on the way to achieving a depth to our experience which on the one hand enables us to understand why we are inclined to feel particular emotions and, on the other hand, invites us to go beyond the rudimentary emotional categories of love and hate to explore the often more subtle but equally powerful emotions that frequently remain unnamed.

Emotions unregistered, unrecognised and unqueried – emotional illiteracy – are costly. They diminish the experience of the individual who, dispossessed of a sufficient emotional repertoire, is ill at ease with her or himself. On the search to soothe or to find what's missing, the individual encounters a range of purported solutions which can be painful and damaging. Food, drugs, violence, fundamentalist religion or fundamentalist politics are at one extreme, while lives lived with little reflection and confidence show the corrosive effects of not understanding much about one's subjective experience. But emotional illiteracy doesn't just affect the individual, sad as that is; it also inhibits or can inhibit the experience of those around them. From having to tread carefully, to being on the receiving end of bullying, the impact of the individual disjointed from her feelings devolves on others who then pick up and sometimes even assume a man- ifestation of the disowned or unprocessed emotions.

At a social level whether at work, in the classroom or in public space, the impact of individuals unable to manage their emotional states reverberates. The manager who is hypercritical diminishes the effectiveness of the group and damages the self- esteem of its members. The distressed child who continually disrupts the class makes it hard for other children to pursue their curiosities. The politician who can't ever be wrong makes it difficult for his researchers to have confidence in their own conclusions.

At a public level, our inability to take account of the com- plexity of our emotional responses to public events and the private feelings we bring to them can leave us with discussions that are just too thin and untextured, reducing public discourse to an unwarranted simplicity where the only possible responses are agreement or adversary. It is not easy to include subtlety and questioning in public conversation. Indeed we are not accus- tomed to it; we have come to rely on summary. But that doesn't mean that we can afford to abandon the attempt. A goal of emotional literacy in public life is to expand what it is possible to consider in the public realm and how it is possible to think and discuss the issues before us. Emotional literacy enables us to realise on what basis we come to our opinions, why we make the decisions we do and why we defend the positions we take in the way that we do. As many of the pieces in this collection propose, public conversation – and hence our private and public lives – would be enhanced if we could underpin the move away from the simplicity of adversary towards the acceptance of multiple voices and intricacy.

Emotional literacy is in no way a substitute for a political programme. Nor is it a guide to living. Like reading, writing and arithmetic, it is a tool and a potential source of deep creativity. Without a knowledge of words, narrative and the capacity to analyse text or the ability to manipulate numbers, we cannot communicate or create. Without a knowledge of our emotions, their trajectories and transformations, we can't hope to mature or to think more profoundly about what motivates us, our desires, and what stands in the (emotional) way of their satisfactions. I hope that these pieces, originally written for the *Guardian* over the last few years, will demonstrate how emotional literacy can be applied to private and public life and stimulate others to engage in this project.

Hidden Truths

Uneasy with Tears

It is not the tears of hurt, of grief, of pain, of shame or of anger that perplex. Those tears we instinctively understand. Feelings that are often too big to be contained by words saturate the body and seep out, crystallising and enunciating the hurt. Words just won't do. But what are we to make of the tears that come involuntarily, unexpectedly and, apparently, paradoxically? We make love and cry. We feel on the verge of being understood and we weep. Mandela is released and tears pour down our face. These tears tell a different story.

What about the weepies? Where do they fit in? What about our propensity to cry at poignancy? So much of our cultural production goes for an emotional jugular based not on trauma, drama or tragedy, but on the reunification of man and woman, mother and daughter, separated friends, fractured families, divided countries, self-respect regained. What inclines us to cry then? And what about the fact that those tears are cried in dark theatres, shielded from others?

Tears are how babies show their need and hurt. Hunger, discomfort, loneliness, tiredness, terror are deciphered by the grown-up in charge, responded to, and the baby feels soothed. Encircled by sure arms, the baby relaxes as its signals are recognised and understood. The weeping ceases, the baby settles, equilibrium is restored.

Tears – as a precursor to language – occupy the emotional space between self and other. If the baby's tears are not shunned, but recognised and accepted, the baby learns that its gestures will be responded to. What it feels, which is after all, who it is, is alright. The tears announce a need which later will be traced – both more subtly and more explicitly – through words, body movement and expression. But for the moment, tears enter and shape that space between the baby and the world outside, articulating desire, hurt, need and the search for comfort.

In time, language and physical mastery extend the child's communicative range. Tears now express frustration. When a toddler can't manage to do something, it is as though there is a fierce blow, an emotional insult, to its sense of self. Tears are like the crumple zone. The child's frustration folds in on itself and the child collapses. It is almost unbearable to watch the gap the child experiences between its desire and the execution of that desire. The rawness of that gap makes us uncomfortable. From our discomfort, we feel protective. But, if the child won't let us comfort it, we may find ourselves trying to chivvy it out of its feeling. The child's tears remind us of the injury frustration brings to a little one's self-esteem.

The helplessness and frustration that lurk behind the grand ideas of childhood begin to lessen in time and tears become more discriminating. Children cry when they are physically hurt, when they are homesick or when they are ashamed. It's not that they don't feel deep sadness, sorrow and grief; they do, and they will cry when they have those emotions. But childhood is a time of learning – when it is and when it isn't all right to cry. Children take their lead from their parents and peer group. Parents can feel that it is wrong to cry (actually to hurt or suffer) in front of their children. They conceal their tears, disguise them as a sniffle, ensure that their tears are not a burden to their children. We may agree with this, but children may gather from the absence of adult tears that there is shame about crying, especially for big boys who don't – or shouldn't.

We tend to shy away from, and are uneasy with, tears. It seems they are all right if we can cajole the other out of them, and if we can extend a protectiveness to the crier. But tears can make us uncomfortable if they seem to present a demand. We can feel awkward and embarrassed when someone around us cries, as if there is something we should do but we don't know what. Staying calm, offering empathy and compassion is often outside our emotional repertoire. We want to act – to relieve the pain – but as we try, we are made aware of our own sadnesses. And, in so far as our own personal grief has not been given expression, we may rush to comfort in a way that stops the tears of the other, not realising how the tears which wash out of one can be very healing.

Tears can alarm if they are not viewed as an expression of pain being engaged; if they are not allowed and received by another. Then, they will be felt as humiliation – an expression of a dreaded vulnerability. If a child cries and is censoriously given a hankie, with the implication that they shouldn't cry, then the child absorbs the idea that she or he shouldn't weep. They adapt to that message and then only cry under extreme duress. In this case, their tears aren't so much a discharge as a stepping stone to further humiliation; a feeling that they have exposed the most shameful aspects of themself.

There is yet another way in which the uncried tears of the beholder work to silence the crier. Tears can be experienced as infectious, as though they will induce an epidemic of crying: 'Don't cry, you'll start the others off.' Are tears really so dangerous that they mustn't be started off in others? What is it that they contain that they are so easy to evoke and yet must be avoided?

Tears represent our profound connections with one another as well as our separateness from each other. They are an acute expression of this tension: our individuality – that is to say, how we in our marrow experience things – and our essential attachments, the web of relations that makes us uniquely who we are. Tears are like a connective tissue, stamped with our own personality, but stimulated by emotion created in the human family.

We cry most poignantly, then, when we are moved. Not when hurt has only been enunciated, but when hurt is seen and then released. When a tension which has been unbearable and unresolved dissolves, the emotionally tight way in which one has held oneself gives way. The unshed tears of previous hurt, which have calcified the heart, now flow, melting the barriers, bathing the heart and reopening it.

*

Recognition, understanding and love are the principal emotional scenarios that provoke tears of poignancy. They are fuelled by a cycle that starts with a love (or self-regard) and turns to disappointment and misunderstanding. Marooned in this disappointment or misunderstanding, the person becomes isolated. They may feel anger or resentment, despair or hopelessness. They are cut off from the other save through conflict.

The tears come, not most intensely from the conflict but from the remaking of the connection. When the misunderstandings are unravelled, when personal pride is restored, or when the acceptance one has imagined is lost is instead visibly offered. Acceptance, recognition, reconnection, love, repair, resolution, forgiveness, are the emotional states that can make tears flow as hearts release their ache. These powerful states, in which one makes oneself again in connection with another, are the expression of our profound desires to be accepted. Like the baby who finds recognition and acceptance when it cries, whose aloneness dissolves as it reconnects with its carer, grown-up tears of acknowledgement are like the rebalancing of emotional justice – redemptive, cleansing and reforming.

Just Buzzing Doing Nothing

What is laziness? This heavily moralistic word presumes a conscious decision to not do, or to do, what is expected at the minimum rather than the optimum revolutions per minute. Laziness implies a sense of intention. It looks like an obstinate refusal. But what is it that is represented in laziness, and what is going on for the individual who is described or describes herself as lazy?

I think we can get a hint of what is contained in laziness from our responses to the perceived laziness of others. We feel outrage at the 'lazy' person's seeming capacity to get away with something. There is a judgment. How dare they be so self-indulgent? The notion that not to be lazy requires effort is important. It suggests that we operate with a belief that we have to take ourselves by the scruff of the neck in order to counteract this tendency which would otherwise overwhelm us. Partly this is so, but partly it is an upside-down view of laziness. It imputes the laziness to the wrong part of the action.

From the inside of laziness we get a rather different picture about its meanings. Psychic effort can produce a crushing passivity. This hurtful form of laziness is not a refusal to do, but the result of an enormous effort to overcome that which feels so hard to do. The so-called lazy person stands in awe of those who can accomplish, manage, create and fulfil so many tasks. They don't find it within themselves to do such things. The doing of their own tasks often leaves them feeling depleted. It is not that they are luxuriating in oceans of spare energy; rather, that their energy cannot seem to extend to meet their own desired goals.

This is a painful state, akin to what one might feel after a bout of flu. The strength required to manage x or y task simply isn't there. But why not? Is it that some of us are more energetic than others, or is low energy an expression of depression and malaise?

Well-adjusted low energy, in which the person is comfortable with their pace, is of no essential concern. Neither is the laziness which means a kind of giving up, either a conscious or an unwitting abandon. Such laziness can be an enjoyable state. To laze is to bask in a kind of relaxation which derives its pleasures from a sense that it is just on the edge of permissibility. By contrast, the enervated state that shaves off into malaise, and then into a block against activating desire, creates a spiral of debilitation which makes action seem impossible. This is a form of laziness which can be seen as a blocking mechanism that both protects and harms. The malaise makes it impossible to act with enthusiasm because the result of acting or the experience of acting produces more anxiety than not acting.

But what is it that this anxiety blocks? The anxiety is a signal about a threatening psychic state. What is threatened if the person were to act would be a challenge to a self-concept that has come to see itself as passive. Why should this be a problem? Surely activity is more pleasurable and rewarding than passivity? Not necessarily. For a variety of reasons, passivity has become the psychological result of the internalisation of messages about self-identity.

It happens rather like this: a pattern has become established in which a person's original initiatives were disregarded; this happens to all of us some of the time without being troublesome, but the continual thwarting, misreading and ridiculing of initiative creates a sense inside the person that what they produce, what emanates from them, is somehow not quite right. They may try to present themselves and their desires differently and, if they are still not heard or seen, they may get angry, they may withdraw, they may comply and look as though they are not in trouble; they will have absorbed a message that it is better not to show.

This message 'not to show' has to compete with the responses they have to being disregarded. These responses, of anger or of feeling bad, fail to find expression either, and so there is a sense of being doubly disregarded. The psychic energy required to dampen down these double disappointments produces what, on the outside, may look like laziness and passivity, while, on the inside, the person is caught up in the most extraordinary (unconscious) expenditure to bind up their initiatives and capacities and to overcome the sense of shame which has arisen out of their feeling that what they had was wrong – or, at least, not right.

This scenario repeated over time means that someone daren't quite manage to express or act upon what they feel to be inside them. Their preoccupations are diverted to keeping things inside, rather than letting them out. Their apparent laziness is then the outcome of a painful internal struggle, a fear that they will be ignored or judged negatively and that they will be ridiculed for their efforts. Leapfrogging over such internal barriers to acting would release gallons of energy for use by the person, but the inhibition on doing has been internalised.

So a lazy administrator or a lazy child in school may not be skiving off; he or she may be making the most extraordinary efforts to do what they do. They may encounter a set of tasks which they judge to be manageable, but come a cropper when they embark on fulfilling them. They may have plenty of ideas for doing them, but the energy for the tasks drains out of them as they set out to do them. They feel themselves to be disabled; to be pushing the boulder up the mountain, rather than acting on what is before them. They are engaged in a psychodrama in which they are contesting a felt sense of wrongness, of shame, or of potential ridicule or judgment.

The battle inside is mirrored in their relationship to the outside. Their superior at work, their teacher or parent becomes the recipient of the projection that they aren't much good, that they are to be judged, that they are lazy. This felt unfairness inside further depletes them. They are defeated and the release of energy for the tasks seems out of reach. The projection then becomes real. They are seen as lazy. They are judged, and even ridiculed. The possibility of getting out from under this boulder seems impossible.

Laziness, then, is in many ways a seemingly bizarre manifestation of its opposite: busyness. There is so much buzzing inside the person which needs quieting in order just to get on, that they are drained. Their psychic exhaustion results from the attempt to still their initiatives and to protect themselves from the imagined ridicule and shame.

For us to moralise about laziness is, therefore, highly unproductive. It simply speaks to our impatience, rather than recognising psychic pain. What is needed is to develop a compassionate stance that can support the initiatives; to convey to the 'lazy' individual, the 'lazy' schoolchild, that their effort is recognised. This recognition is a first step in helping them release their energy for themself rather than against themself.

Sticking in the Knife

Do you like to be teased? Probably not. Most of us don't. Do you like to tease? Well, that's another story. We almost all indulge in it at some time or another – with nary a thought to its effect on the teased, whether it's a tease with a twinkle or the kind of teasing that's no fun at all.

Between adolescent boys, it's not difficult to figure out what's going on. The teaser alights upon what he perceives as a vulnerability in someone else and goes for it. It is as though, by savaging the other boy, he can hide from the fact that he identifies with that vulnerability. Boys preparing themselves for life sense a need to be hard – therefore, all signs of softness must be banished. God help the kid who questions that assumption, or who exposes the boys' collective weakness. So a child who brings a cuddly bear on a group holiday may be taunted for being babyish; a goalie who lets in lots of goals when playing against a superior, older team may be the focus of teasing – 'you rubbish midget' – from the other players who feel ashamed and battered by defeat by bigger boys and who are looking for some way to soften the blow and deflect blame from themselves.

If the tease works, that's to say if the child is unable to fight back, then it can be employed again and again whenever the boys are confronted with their own vulnerability. Of course, this is a variant of the bullying in schools between teachers and children that occurs less frequently now, but still often enough to alarm. There are many educational situations in which teachers use humiliation to try to keep control. Perhaps the teacher can't get a grip on the situation as they would wish, perhaps their power has been eroded, and so the demeaning tease is wielded as a stick to re-establish power.

In more benevolent situations between adult and children, it is easy to see what stimulates the tease. The child has a particularly engaging mannerism that makes the parents smile. A tease is a way of giving that pleasure back to the child (or so the parents think). But rarely does this attempt to reflect the parents' joy have the intended effect. Rather, the child can feel exposed. The playful light that has been shone on them is too bright. They're not sure what they've done and they feel awkward. Instead of smiling back in recognition of a pleasurable exchange, the child may cry or get angry. What emanates from delight shades into shame.

Curiously, a parent's teasing can go down quite well if it is directed not at some special cuteness, but at a particularly galling habit of the child – such as playing the CD, GameBoy and television all at the same time while trying to carry on a conversation, or contriving never to have the right shoes, book, coat, whatever in the right place at the right time. Perhaps this kind of a tease can be endured and maybe even enjoyed a little because it's a rebuke with a light touch. Better that than a telling-off or a direct put-down.

But what about teasing between adults? Is it a portmanteau stance that can be used to enhance good feelings about specially charming aspects of a person? Is it a way to confront someone with a truth about themselves they won't see? Is it all good fun?

Just as teasing an irritating or perplexing child can be a ploy, so teasing between adults is sometimes a form of negotiating – a way of telling someone something about themselves that it would be too embarrassing to point out to them directly. One can off-load discomfort without engaging in confrontation. And if the person recognises the truth of what's being said about them, it needn't be hurtful, but rather a kind of giggled understanding of an inconvenience. The 'what stands between you' is acknowledged, even if it isn't changed.

If the teasing is not a nicely-judged piece of social interaction, though, what then? What if the teaser realises that the recipient of a tease is close to tears and blunders in with an attempted self-defence – 'It's only a joke, I didn't really mean it'? What provokes the tease and what is its intent? Is it really as free of intended hurt as the perpetrator claims?

Hardly. Even the most sceptical of anti-Freudians can see that Freud was on to something when he revealed the hostility implicit in much of joking. A tease is an underhand way of sticking in the knife, of attacking someone while appearing to make light of it, and of avoiding responsibility for an angry or sadistic intent. The hurt that is caused doesn't have to be considered – if there's a barb embedded in the tease, so what? The teaser feels blameless. It is surely their victim who has taken the thing the wrong way.

But what prompts the tease in the first place? What fuels the hostility? What is the nastiness that is at the heart of a tease? Like the adolescent boys attempting to distance themselves from their own fragility through teasing, the teaser is deeply uneasy with him or herself. They feel angry or insecure, and contempt snuffles up their nostrils. They feel they aren't good enough themselves certainly, but then neither is anyone else. Their antennae seek out their prey – preferably someone whose external persona mirrors some shameful aspect of their own inner self. The self-hatred they feel is encoded in the hostile tease. Like a bullet from one damaged person to another, teasers bolster themselves up at others' expense. They try to pass on to another a hurt that is lodged within. The tease is a dagger. It is not benign. It is the use of another as a dustbin for the dispersal of one's own distress. In the dumping, there is the attempt to achieve personal well-being, to rid oneself of the nasty feelings inside.

We acknowledge the unpleasant side of the sexual tease without too much difficulty. We know we've been toyed with and charmed, not for our benefit but because of the insatiable need of the flirt. We feel the hurt, the outrage even, of being tricked. We may have enjoyed the attention but we have no doubt that the intent is fundamentally hostile and a very long way from a tease with a twinkle. We can feel that behind the 'look but don't touch' is someone for whom others are fodder. Contact is too difficult for them. They can only tease. There's little confusion about this pattern of behaviour; we soon come to recognise it for what it is. So what stops us naming the teaser as offensive – sending back the tease, rather than accepting it?

If we do send the nasty tease back, we are entering into a confrontation. We would be exposing the aggression below the surface. It takes fancy psychic footwork to get over the hurt fast enough, to recognise what has been sent and then to challenge the person without responding in kind. But by not reacting, we are protecting the teaser from acknowledging their own hostility. There follows an implicit collusion between teaser and teased which holds the teaser in a position of power over the teased. Is that how we want it?

The Indiscreet Charm
of the Flirt

O ne of the more delightful aspects of romance is celebrated on Valentine's Day. In the sending of anonymous cards we playfully indulge in the pleasures of flirting. Charms are registered and acknowledged in a hidden form. Flirting, as Adam Phillips has engagingly written, is one of the human gambits – poised between safety and danger – for getting to know another. It can be anything from an expression of mild interest in someone to a playlet of emotional brinksmanship.

There are flirts and flirtees. The positions can be interchangeable and mutual. They may only develop their charms in the presence of a receptive and passive flirtee, or there may be reciprocal flirting. The exchange is a chance to show parts of a self that are often hidden or undeveloped. The flirt finds aspects of himself that he imagines will stimulate the other. For some, the act of flirting is like a play in which the protagonist reinvents the self. The flirt charms the other and simultaneously the self. Flirting can be a part of, or a prelude to, friendship or a love affair. It is not exclusively sexual, although it is often characterised as such.

A welcome act of flirtation can act as a mood elevator, enhancing the recipient's well-being, touching him and making him more receptive, generous and open-minded. The appreciated self expands and melts. In a micro-version of the feelings engendered at the start of a love affair, people become tender and responsive to their environment in general. Unwanted attention, however, in which the flirt has seriously misjudged the reception of their beam on another, can cause great distress with harassment and invasion clouding the space around the individual uneager for such attention.

Flirting is part of the panoply of emotional connection. Like any human gesture, it can contain within it both the wish for contact as well as a fear of it. But, while much of flirting is benign, what can we say about the compulsive flirt, the man or woman unable to seek or find engagement except via flirting? What motivates and drives that form of connection? And what are the effects of that kind of flirting on others? Can it be damaging to agent and recipient alike?

The habitual flirt, who rivets their attention on another in such a way that they feel a special and intimate connection has been made, seeks an intensity of contact. This contact may be unsustainable in a primary relationship or, even if it exists, it may fail to meet the flirt's needs sufficiently for continuously heightened emotional experience. The flirt may be an intensity junkie who requires someone outside him or herself to be preoccupied with. The intensive interest in another is used to get away from a self that feels barren. By fixing upon another, and by inducing the other similarly to fix back, the emptiness is temporarily eased by the reflection. The flirt creates the interest and attention in her or himself which they then use to feed a void.

But because the void cannot be addressed in a contact that is essentially self-involved rather than truly related, the genuine attention that the flirt may elicit is not usable and therefore wasted. The separate incidents which make up the flirting keep the person's emotional starter motor going and revved up, but eventually the energy drains away because the relationship that need, to evolve out of such contact can't be managed. Empty, once again, because the contact that has been created is autistic rather than relational, the person suffers the loss of what they had deemed was a potentially salvationary relationship. They feel compelled to search for someone else through whom they can restart a cycle in which they display and are then momentarily filled up by a promised capacity for love, intensity and passion.

Repetitive flirting driven by such motivation is an enactment of a painful emotional scenario for the individual. The person longing for contact pursues another by flattering them and disclosing their most attractive self. The attention is temporarily taken up and enjoyed and in those moments the hopes for a mutual relationship are raised. But, just as the contact seems within reach, it is clipped one way or another and the contact is thwarted. The flirting person has managed to captivate another only to find their interest in the other then vaporises. The enjoyment of self and other can only be felt in snippets and the intensity of the momentary exchange becomes the stand-in for a sustained relationship.

For some this scenario is dangerously extended so that the relationships of potential support and love are threatened. James, while living with and loving Sam, would be passionately drawn to other men in ways that endangered his relationship. Through covert trysts and the exchange of secrets, James created new intimacies which, by their specialness and urgency, threatened his relationship with Sam. James only feels alive when he lives on the edge, threatening that which he has built up. The wish to be transported elsewhere, to find himself in a new life, to force his relationship with Sam to the brink, gives him a sense of being alive in two ways. The pull between Sam and the other object of his interest is a powerful emotional bolt, exciting and energising him and making him alert and lively. As he feels his desire for these two men and feels their desire of him, he experiences himself both as a wanted person as well as someone full of desire himself. These feelings combine to produce in himself a sense of a psychological crusade for himself. He and his desires are centre-stage and for a short period he feels not empty and barren but full of his own cause.

But his sorties into other relationships also produce feelings of guilt, which then lead him to withdraw and create emotional havoc in others. Sadly, the attention he has lavished on others and tried to enjoy for himself rebounds, making him feel that his desires can only produce destructive ends. He replays a story in which his wanting is not only dashed, but is hurtful to himself and others.

Repetitive flirts may be re-enacting a felt emotional truth that for them love and intimacy cannot be maintained. This painful scenario can only be turned around when the person can risk abandoning the flirt in order to trust a different, less intense and more sustained form of engagement.

The Truth in the Lie

Behind the *Guardian* questionnaire's 'when do you lie?' is an honest recognition of the prevalence of lying in everyday life. Lying is a mechanism for greasing the social wheels, for avoiding unnecessary hurt and for allowing decisions to be taken without consultation. And yet, although lying is endemic, we tend to be uncomfortable about it. Our discomfort inclines us to pretty up the process by grading deceit. We tell white lies; we are economical with the truth; we ridicule the naïvety of those whose morality is offended by lying.

It is the discomfort that intrigues me. Lying appears to be a prosaic feature of life, but it is cast as moral failure and carries the weight of disapproval. Why do we live with such a disjuncture? What does it express?

The disjuncture is related to what engenders lying. It feels easier to lie than to work out a way to give a proper account of oneself. We don't refuse a dinner invitation when we discover who the other guests are by laboriously talking our potential host through our own processes of wishing they hadn't invited people we find particularly irksome. We say, we are sorry to decline but we are busy. We find it difficult to say that we are not able to come without concealing or revealing why. We give a false explanation because we assume an explanation is required. Our guilt at acting on our own desire often propels us into a lie, rather than a simple statement of unavailability.

But perhaps no explanation is required. Perhaps what we are unused to doing – namely being straightforward – feels too difficult, so we avoid it. We misconstrue what is required of us. Instead of saying no thanks, we soften the no by seeking approval. We cast ourselves in a less defined and more acceptable light, both to our friend and to ourself.

This kind of lying is pragmatic rather than wilful. We excuse ourselves because it isn't very important. Depending on our sensibility we may feel uneasy, squirm inside, assure ourselves that we won't put ourselves through lying again or simply rationalise the lie. We can be outraged, however, when we encounter lies at work, in local or national government, at the bank or in school. Lies perpetrated in institutional settings are tinged with something sinister. They are threatening because they undermine a trust between the individual and the public institution. The deviousness required to concoct and carry out a public lie is laid bare. It offends the notion that we are co-operating as a culture. Although it exposes the cowardice of the institution, it also induces feelings of individual impotence. One's rage feels useless in the face of premeditated deceit.

But what of the person who simply can't help lying, who

finds it difficult to give an account of himself or herself that is narratively accurate? Richard is a 35-year-old dentist whose daily activities fail to interest him. He feels dull, empty and boring. He can't imagine that anyone will be interested in him as he is barely interested in himself. He invents for himself a life which involves danger and challenge. In recounting his fabricated existence he engenders concern from others and feels himself to be less of an outsider.

His invented life, his compulsive lying works on one level. It does engage the interest of others. He gets a kind of contact. But the contact is bittersweet for it bypasses a more authentic engagement and leaves him further alienated from others. While he has invented stories to draw others to him, once there, they are not much use to him as real companions because privately he ridicules them as gullible and untrustworthy.

Richard is compelled to lie to create a sense of value in himself. But a peculiar aspect of his duplicity is that while on one level it distances him from his experience, at another there is an emotional truth within his fabrications. The stories and mysteries he constructs resonate with emotional states he can't get access to directly. The barren, empty, dull world he lives in is only one side of the story. His emptiness co-exists with emotional dramas that preoccupy him, but for which he has found few pathways to express.

Lying for Richard is an act of creation. It gives him a chance to play out different selves, to give imaginative expression to the parts of him that aren't in the least boring. He tries on these 'invented selves' and experiences some relief that he has a rich and imaginative life inside him. Lying, for him, is masquerade in preparation for life. His struggle is to invert the sham; to face the emptiness and reclaim the energy and imaginative powers invested in his constructions.

To turn from Richard's involuntary lying to the more commonplace, we can readily observe that children try out lying as a part of their repertoire. Children have many ingenious routes for not doing what irks them. They don't hear what is asked of them, they refuse to absorb what they are being told, they harness our smiles by charmingly wriggling out of a difficulty; and when these routes fail, they may proffer a lie. Usually a tease or a wink that lets them know that we know is enough to let them off the hook of the lie. Being caught into maintaining a lie produces considerable discomfort and a child whose lies are not penetrated is a worried child. It is confused about its own power. It is confused about how much it needs to be in charge. It is confused by grown-ups who don't challenge. If children start to lie habitually, we need to listen carefully because it usually means that they are in quite a muddle and can't find a way to get out of it.

Like Richard, a child who is habitually lying is finding an indirect route to express him or herself. The child feels unable to reveal itself, to disclose what has actually happened, sometimes out of a fear of being misunderstood, sometimes out of a fear of punishment and sometimes because it doesn't know how to declare its dissent and be heard. In the last case, the lying is not so much about deceit as it is to protect the child's wishes. The child feels thwarted and conceals what it has done.

But the commonest type of lying children engage in is around aggrandisement. It is a sop to feelings of confusion when the game is unclear but the currency is bigger, better, more. Sometimes the bigger, better, more is about who one's parents are, sometimes about the size of one's rubber collection and sometimes about the type of monsters that have been visiting one at night. Lying in these cases is about mastery and positioning. Employed occasionally it shouldn't cause much concern. But a child who unceasingly brandishes tall stories has something big to tell us about how little he or she feels. Rather than scold or poo-poo them we need to take the emotional veracity of their story seriously and help them deconstruct the narrative into the emotional truth it contains.

Don't Tell Anyone, But . . .

Gossip occurs whenever people come together. Veiled as shop talk, or catching up, it has a particularly indulgent, slightly naughty, delicious feel to it, like going to the movies in the morning. Gossip is aligned to curiosity, and indeed some have said that psychoanalysis is the professionalisation of gossip, elevating to a craft the practice of taking apart one's attitudes towards another or others.

But gossip has another function. Like the put-down, it is a displacement of distress, and this is done both publicly and privately. I want to explore both the more benevolent aspects of gossip and its role in helping us place ourselves in our interpersonal worlds, as well as to look at the more malicious aspects. So first, to the positive or, to be more accurate, less problematic aspects of gossip.

Gossip is a mechanism we use in response to the inevitable

separateness of our individual lives. In scrutinising the actions and attitudes of others, we are expanding our experiences by trying to enter into and understand the goings-on of others. In making a canvas broader than that of our own limited experience, we use others' experiences as frames of reference.

When we gossip about someone's behaviour or action we are sifting through those areas, criticising some and approving others. We are mapping out territories which we think it appropriate to evaluate. But this is also about evaluating ourselves. 'If we were in so-and-so's shoes,' we think, 'we would/wouldn't act that way.' It is not so much that we are engaged in high-handed moralism. Rather it's a process of discovery: 'Would I be like Fiona and run off and have an affair and leave enough clues so that my lover found out, or would I . . .?' This form of gossip is essentially benign. It is about finding out about ourselves by dissecting the lives of others.

We are also, of course, trying to work out how another person lives their life. Often we are in wonderment about how someone leads a life so very differently from ours. We may admire their difference or feel tantalised by what they are able to do. We may, of course, disapprove or feel threatened. The act of gossip allows us to imagine and even understand different ways of doing things.

If we are generous, we gossip about a stingy person because it is so incomprehensible to us. We can't understand what motivates it or why. In gossip, we not only condemn them but we look at their meanness from many angles, attempting to penetrate the unfathomable. In the case of someone who thinks they would never consider having an affair but gossips avidly about an acquaintance who is doing so, we might understand that the gossiper comes into contact with a part of themselves that could also act in a similar manner and have a clandestine affair.

Indeed, it may emerge that what makes gossip enticing is an unrecognised part of oneself in the other. Vicariously trying out what we disown by focusing on the action in someone else, we reiterate the gossip as we try to familiarise ourself with the disassociated part of ourself.

At the same time, of course, the gossip is an attempt to create a boundary between ourself and the behaviour of the other. We disparage their action and thus reinforce how unacceptable it would be for us. The act of gossiping, with its criticisms and disavowals, binds up our own ambivalence by casting certain fantasies or longings outside permissible bounds.

This attempt to separate ourself off from another also comes into play when we gossip about an acquaintance whom we judge has betrayed us. We try to unload the hurt by discussing what they have done and, as we differentiate ourself from them, we discover our own values. We are creating the boundaries which we are loath to traverse.

But what about gossip that is, in its intent, an attack? What motivates the poisonous sting of such gossip and what kind of need is it being asked to answer? A common denominator may well be a felt sense of inadequacy which is relieved by making an attack on someone else.

A competent woman architect suffered from egregious attacks by those who envied her. Others in her office and field would run her down, although her actions were scrupulous. Her crime was her capability, and her detractors' incompetence with handling their envy of her. While their gossiping helped them feel better briefly, by criticising her, it didn't address their personal disappointment and their difficulty in accepting or changing their own situations.

The gossip soon became the gloss over what was becoming a bitterness towards their own lives, while the emotional energy spent gossiping shored up their envy and sense of inadequacy. The gossip united them in a club of fellowship, but in doing so it excluded her and removed them from getting what they could from her. It demarcated a territory which, like the hurtful games of childhood, barred the one who, for whatever reason, disturbed the equilibrium. In fact, they needed to pinpoint their own strengths and assess what they wanted to develop in themselves rather than use her as the butt of their distress.

Finally, there is a neither benevolent nor malign form of gossip which functions in the public sphere. Here, we can talk about people who are total strangers to us, yet who inhabit our lives through their fame. Via the pages of our newspapers and magazines and through radio and television chat shows, we engage in mass conversation concerning people we know nothing about. The gossip dispensed is tailored for different social groups and is an indulgence shared by millions.

We can all have an opinion on Prince Charles or Tony Blair, not an opinion based on their work or craft, but about the perception we are offered about the conduct of their lives. This rather ridiculous recreation we partake in – which can arouse a good deal of passion – makes sense if we understand it as a way in which we are minimising the alienating and often fragmented aspects of our own lives.

Gossiping with a group of people about someone who is both visible and yet, in essence, unknown, brings us together. It bridges some of the divide that exists between us and makes a stab at the features of intimacy present in a smaller society. We create and then appropriate larger-than-life figures to idealise, criticise and link us. Where God's messengers were once the method of connecting us, we now create movie stars, celebrities, supermodels, writers and politicians as social adhesion.

But the way we adhere through them is not so much by adulation or even simple admiration. It is through the dissection of the ordinary aspects of their lives, about which, in truth, we really know very little. As we gossip about their 'private lives' we rehumanise them and make ourselves part of an emotional global village.

The Put-Down

A t the heart of many casual acquaintanceships is the curious phenomenon of the put-down. In order to connect with one another, two people – unclear about what they have in common or unsure about how and what to talk about with one another – discover with relief that they share knowledge of a third person. Proceeding to put that person down or gossip in a way which, while not quite malicious, is less than generous, they create a bond between them; they may then go on to put down other mutual friends or unknown people, thus marking their acquaintanceship with a pretend intimacy because they have entered into infelicitous territory with one another.

Why is this mechanism so inviting? What is it about gossip in this form that seems to provide an access point for pseudo intimacy? And why is the put-down in general such an easy, almost natural way in which we deal with one another? What

are we escaping from in ourselves when we repeatedly or gratu-
itously put down others? What are we saying about how we
regard relations between ourself and others? Why do we sacri-
fice a rational, more rounded, sense of another by resorting to
a fairly cheap shot?

Of course, hierarchy marks and structures many of our relationships. We stratify one another without much awareness. We
assess for class, warmth, beauty, integrity, wit, agility, accomplishment, maternality, and so on. In the microsecond that we
rank in this way, we are placing in order to make sense, to fit the
person into the pattern of the world as we have construed it.
And as we incorporate that new person into our world – 'they're
like this, so I can understand and accommodate them' – so we
simultaneously reposition ourselves *vis-à-vis* them and the internal charts we carry about how things are between people. But if
we slow the process down we might ask why making common
cause with one person involves putting down a third party.
What motivates this peculiar form of bonding which is so
endemic that even those with great integrity will indulge?

The most benevolent interpretation could be that we are
revealing what is usually hidden: a nasty bit of ourselves. We are
thus giving our new acquaintance a chance to see what we are
really like – not only the sociable, friendly exterior, but a human
being who is capable of enjoying the seedy.

However, I am not sure that this is a sufficient explanation.
I fear that the put-down reveals an acceptance of a process that
relies on lassitude. We find it taxing to confront the awkwardness of a new social encounter. That discomfort combines with
an emotional ineptitude and leads us to rely on the mechanism
of dumping negative feelings about another as a short-cut. We

displace our unease by ridiculing something about another, and feel better because we've discharged our discomfort. Our new acquaintance joins us in the effort and so we are legitimated in the practice.

But perhaps this is all really innocuous and you will read these comments of mine as the rather ridiculous meanderings of those of us whose activity it is to wander into the minutiae of meaning of the everyday. Does it really matter if we create a temporary feeling of closeness through exclusion and put-down? Does it really harm anyone?

The harm it does is, of course, not only to the party who has been gossiped about; rather, it is to the pair who off-load together in this rather lazy way, who are now far from understanding what they feel uncomfortable about and why they bond on this basis.

Meeting someone new holds the promise of connection; the experience of being understood afresh, of accounting for oneself, one's interests, passions and dislikes from a perspective which, without the baggage of prehistory, can be illuminating and pleasurable. One has a chance to make a relationship without the preconceptions that all existing or well-established friendships rely on. In addition, a new friend has the potential to open up different aspects of the world; their attitudes and their perspective are not sodden with well-known assumptions.

But these potentials can be hard to realise. Instead of the openness required to engage with someone new, one lapses into the tired territory of one's own criticalness and, in offering that as a point of contact, perhaps unwittingly forecloses new experience, because there is little space to hear about the other's, or to show one's personal enjoyment. The embarrassment and excitement that could characterise a new encounter therefore collapses.

And what about the more common and equally frequent process of putting down others when they have no obvious connection to the issue at hand, when they are, without cause, called in to take the blame? I'm thinking now of the way in which – when for example we misplace the dictionary – we blame the children/wife/cleaner. When we hurt ourselves, we can seek to assign culpability to another. When we are helpless in the face of random violence, we demonise youth. When we fail to get what we want, we can fixate on another's good fortune.

This kind of off-loading would seem to answer a different psychological problem. When we are unable to sustain directly the annoyance we've encountered (one which we may have caused), or when we are confused about the basis of our irritation, we seek to disperse and make it someone else's responsibility. By bringing another into it (even if only in our heads) we create both a cause and a witness. If it weren't for them, we wouldn't be annoyed. Their participation (silent and unknown) in our dramalette validates our own experience. To bear it without off-loading it on to another would be to take a kind of emotional responsibility for the irritation, the hurt or the grievance – something we are frequently unable to do because of the repeated ignominy of ignored childhood hurts.

So when we take someone's name in vain, when we try to make ourselves better through toppling another's character, reputation or good fortune, we are plundering our relationships in order to give ourselves relief from a felt sense of internal injury. Such injuries, engendered by minor irritations, awkward social encounters or hurts, speak to our refusal to accept helplessness.

We continue to protest and fight that helplessness through off-loading.

Engaging with the hurt and helplessness directly and quietly ourself might be a more productive enterprise. If we were to prise open the space where we habitually dump on another and directly soothe our own hurt, the balm of attention might console us more successfully than the compulsion to discharge.

None of this is to say that taking someone's name in vain or gossiping could, or should, be defined in moral terms. Gossip, especially, can sometimes have a delicious feel. It can be a way to release hurts which are specifically engendered by competitiveness or excluding behaviours. But that's another issue.

The Need not to Know

How are we to understand denial? We all have a propensity to deny what we know, whether it is ignoring 10-year-old warnings on BSE, forgetting about the swelling in a breast, living in a dead relationship, or walking around as though the vast inequities we see are a law of nature rather than manufactured. We seal off the unwanted from ourselves until that moment when it pops out again and the horror of confronting what is becomes inescapable.

There are two processes involved in denial. One is a form of repression, getting whatever is troublesome out of one's mind: an interesting question being, where does it go and how does it get to where it's going? The other way is failing to remember, which offers another interesting question: what makes it hard to remember what we know and what we've seen and experienced or been told, what intervenes to *stop* us retaining and recalling that which it may be important to remember?

The thirteenth-century etymological root of denial is 'saying no to'. This sense of active refusal has been reinvented to the ungainly phrase 'I was in denial.' The self can manage to know only what sits in certain compartments and not others. To be 'in denial' is to be unable to link up the compartments.

What leads us to deny is the unbearable nature of knowing. Adults who have survived terrifying experiences in childhood that threatened their sanity have often done so only at the cost of dissociating – seeing themselves as outside the situation of terror as it was happening. They found – or, one might say, created – another self (maybe multiple selves) who acted as an observer or witness; a self who saw but was somehow unaffected. In this process, the feelings that the terrorised child experienced are sealed off from consciousness along with that child who lived through the violence. The child's invented self continues on less harmed because it has only seen, rather than gone through, the dreadful time.

We can all, in a way, understand this mechanism because we've tasted it in some form or other when endangered. But the inability to hold on to information about the everyday – our poisoned planet, worrying changes in our body states, a personal reliance on drugs or sensation, or the bad relationship one is stuck in – seems hazier. It is a state we slip into rather than an active exit we make. Unpalatable, frightening, challenging information overwhelms, so we 'forget it', we put it 'out' of our minds.

That sense of being overwhelmed and helpless is the very thing that we humans in the West hate. Above all, we are into activity and mastery. We have come to see ourselves as rational, as capable of making informed decisions on our own behalf. So, could it be that when we feel inadequate to the task – when we just don't know what to do, how to proceed, and it all feels too much – we send the unbearableness off into a hidden realm where we hope it won't disturb?

John Southgate, a colleague of mine, has come up with an important way to understand these splitting mechanisms. He argues that multiple personality is the name of the game as far as the psyche goes. We all contain within us many different selves, and we can't avoid compartmentalising and splitting off bits. But the question is how to get these different bits to associate. He argues that mental health can't be defined so much in terms of whether we have different selves, but whether they communicate and associate with one another.

A friend in a loveless – worse, a hopeless – marriage put her denial this way: 'As long as I am angry in this marriage, I can hope and pretend that it will change. I can kick up a fuss and still feel like I am a person with wants that might be manageable, they just don't happen to be being met. It's much easier for me to be angry than to face the incredible longing. That really overcomes me. It's much too painful to take on and I don't know what to do about that.'

Not so different from the Beef Crisis. Talking with people about why the BSE news was so shocking to them, they said it was because, as they readily admitted, a part of them knew already, and couldn't bear to know. If the beef is infected, what of the lamb still carrying the effects of Chernobyl's radiation, the chicken salmonella, the vegetable pesticides, the water nitrates? There is nothing to do but throw up their hands helplessly. But feeling overwhelmed, feeling helpless is not an option. It feels too out of control, as though to recognise the ways in which one is a passive victim (of agribusiness, of environmental catastrophe) is impossible. They must either transform that immediately by feeling guilty about what they have done to the planet – as though they are personally implicated – or there is just so much difficult information coming in that it has to be set aside. The feeling of being a helpless victim has to be suppressed, and to do that the information must be denied.

But what if the information were retained? If the helpless feelings were lived with even if there were no immediate solutions? One of psychoanalysis's contributions is to show that when fear or anxiety overwhelms us, thinking stops. Defence structures narrow the channels into which we allow our thoughts to go. But if we can pause, take a deep psychological breath and try to bear the feelings of helplessness, and not reject them as we feel impelled to do, then thinking needn't stop.

Our mental apparatus may gasp at the enormity of what we are surrendering to. We may try very hard to act to make ourselves feel effective, rather than tolerate what can be overwhelming. But if we can just hang in there, our thinking individually and together will come back to us and we will discover that we can manage more complexity, that difficulty needn't lead only to denial or paralysis.

Facing the feelings of being overwhelmed and helpless makes it possible to remember. If we remember, we can rework, revise and continue to think. If we can't remember, we are in far greater danger of repeating in order to reinstate a part of ourselves that we have lost. We then can retrieve parts of ourselves only through repetition rather than through remembrance. Unless we can acknowledge that certain experiences make us *feel* helpless, we will in fact *be* helpless. Denial locks us into helplessness, whereas a recognition of our feelings of helplessness might free us to engage the world, wearing fewer blinkers.

Running on Empty

Simon was bored. He started ringing up people, looking for some action, somewhere to go. Julie was at her desk, surrounded by piles of work she couldn't pull herself away from. Geoff woke up next to a woman he didn't recognise, felt sick and got the hell out of her flat. Jess, plagued by feelings of emptiness, was ever helpful, stepping in and giving before you even realised you had the need. Cass had a things-to-do list that never ended. All perfectly routine activities, descriptions of daily life.

Overworking, doing lots of sex, or drugs, or compulsive socialising, eating, giving – almost any driven activity – can be an attempt to accommodate what feels like a void, an emptiness at the centre of one's life. We could describe it as the malaise of our time: the reverberation of the empty echo sitting at the core of so much of life.

The paucity of significant meanings and connections can make it hard to place our lives either in the wider world or in the centre of our own existence. As we approach the end of the century, many theories vie for the ultimate explanation of what's wrong with contemporary life and values. We'll see critiques of the secular life, even more proliferation of the nostalgic family that never was, a political agenda, 'Beyond left and right', descending from the Academy. Physicists' theoretical musings will be offered with the so-called Theory of Everything set out to charm us. Fasting, cleansing, chanting, 12-step lookalike programmes will saturate personal life. Grand theories will attempt to ground us by occupying that vacant space where the fragments don't quite connect.

It's tempting to see the social and personal ennui as one and the same – to hope that salvation on either front will rescue the other, that a meaning gained in the social world will ameliorate disquiet in the personal, that private redemption, integrity, doing one's bit honestly, will purify the stench in the world. But although feelings and actions are connected to the wider world, and vice versa, neither can be simplistically reduced to the other. A personal solution to the emptiness inside may not make it any easier to live in a world with so much incongruity. It may even make it more discordant in a different way, drawing a line between inner dissatisfactions, restlessness and frustrations, and the alienation in and from public space.

It is that emptiness inside which can inaugurate a therapy. The sense that whatever one does, one can't quite get it right for oneself; that the strings of a life don't knit together as they should; that there is an incapacity to engender something sustaining from within.

Psychotherapy can't solve the problems of the world – it's not designed to address them – but it does look at how we relate to ourselves and to each other, to what goes on in our private worlds, and it engages with the difficulties, including the gnawing feelings of emptiness, that can beset one there.

In other words, psychotherapy can dare to go where other ways of thinking and experiencing do not. It can enter into the ordinary, murky unease without being frightened or distracted. Anxiety and listlessness – which often underlie the frantic activities of those who work, play or drug themselves superintensively – are the kinds of feelings analysts are used to exploring, to sitting with, in order to work out with their analysands what states of mind create such distress and how to shift them.

What therapy tries to do, if it's any good, is to use the shortish-term relationship – the act of faith the analysand makes in giving over to the therapy relationship – to create an emotional environment where the hole can be experienced and examined, understood and transformed.

The corrosive emptiness which is so voracious that it has had to be sated by sex, food, drugs, work or giving, is often found to be not so much an emptiness – for emptiness is not so hard to satisfy; it can be filled – as a black hole which conceals a sense of disintegration, a dispersing of self. The atomised bits can't seem to connect in a sufficiently meaningful way to generate a sense of sustainable self. The bits can't connect because they themselves make up a gossamer-like shield, covering not an empty core but a core infected with a sense of its own badness.

Beyond Geoff, Simon, Cass and Julie's holes lie feelings of badness, of wrongness, of not being fundamentally all right.

These feelings – harder to bear than the emptiness – are not only hard to bear but can nullify almost any effort the person makes to appease them. Whatever Julie creates of value can become valueless in the face of her core feeling of badness. However much caring Jess gives, she can't quite soothe herself. However much loving Geoff seeks and receives, it can't quite penetrate him deeply enough to make things feel reliably good inside. However much action Simon gets or however many lists Cass generates and completes, dread lies in the in-between moments.

Cruelly, it is in the psyche's attempt to evacuate itself of the bad feelings that the feelings of emptiness are created, and with it the feelings that whatever one has – a good relationship, interesting work, lovely friends – are simply stuck-ons rather than central, absorbing aspects of a life.

But where does that leave us? Why is badness such a compelling psychic state? Why do we gravitate so easily and unconsciously to coalesce a sense of self around a core of bad? Where does bad come from, and where can it be made to go?

Psychotherapy is not so much about turning bad feelings into good ones as about staying with and accepting the bad feelings long enough to make a personal sense of them. Where emotional battering (by the self or another) or flight have been the main options, a setting where we need not run away from bad feelings paradoxically makes them manageable and less insistent.

In therapy, the feeling of badness can be shown to another. It can then be acknowledged and received by the therapist, who can see that this feeling does, for the present, represent the person's truth about her or himself. With that 'truth' accepted between them and not absconded from, the psyche is less frantic: it is believed, which brings a deep relief. Now the person can yield to the many other perceptions she or he holds about her or himself. The badness no longer constitutes the complete story, a story so awful that it has had to be defended against. Instead of the badness being projected, disavowed or drowned out, it becomes a part of the self that can be looked at, felt and made some sense of.

It's possible, then, not to experience oneself as a gaping mouth gobbling up life and people, but to see life as a place in which to express one's complexity.

Revenge

He drove around the streets determined to find the two 16-year-olds. Like a man possessed, he had no thoughts beyond revenge. He saw himself pulling those young things by the scruffs of their necks, forcing them to bend over, pushing their heads together, making them squirm, shaming them. He wanted them to suffer. He wanted them not just to apologise, he wanted them never to forget; not to be able to walk away from the injury they had inflicted. He wanted them to know how it felt.

The odd thing was that Tony wasn't accustomed to feeling vengeful. In fact, he was known for his generosity. When things went wrong, he was inclined to see the other person's point of view; it wasn't an effort for him. Even when people were malicious, he could usually find a way of explaining their actions with a certain sympathy. This equanimity extended to his personal life, where he was a warm and present father, friend and lover. That's what made this desire for a ruthless pursuit of revenge so uncharacteristic and distasteful to him.

His ten-year-old twins had been mugged by the neighbourhood toughs. The tactics his children had used to avoid the area where these kids hung out had been effective in the short term, but finally the inevitable had happened and they couldn't keep the big kids off them. Tony had been attentive to his boys' struggles; coming from the streets himself, he knew something about the options. He knew racism might be involved, since he and his kids were black and the bullies white. He knew that the bullies might be victims themselves – perhaps they, too, were being bullied.

These explanations held. Up to a point. But Tony had warned the big kids not to mess with the younger ones, and when he felt his ability to protect them had been compromised, he flipped into a revenge fantasy that didn't stop until he was out hunting for the bullies.

What distressed him over and above the mugging of his sons was the flood of sadism that accompanied his wish for revenge: the desire to hurt the perpetrators. But his vengeful fantasies weren't that unusual. We tend to take revenge for granted, and many of our plays and movies use it as a theme. We have homilies which try to modify children's desires for retaliatory revenge, indicating that we accept that vengeance is ubiquitous while simultaneously trying to channel it more constructively.

What seems to be at work in revenge is that it is a response to the violation of a boundary – the streets, one's body, one's children – that was, until that moment, marked off as a safe area. Something precious has been stolen. Tony never thought he would be unable to protect his children, especially when they were as young as ten. Sure, he knew about racism and bullying – he had experienced enough of it himself – but the notion that some big boys could nullify his capacity to protect his own children was an intolerable violation. It was out of this violation, the helplessness and the sense that his ability to protect his children had been stolen from him, that his desire for revenge was fuelled.

Revenge is a great mobiliser. It inverts the humiliation caused by an undefended attack. By visiting hurt on the perpetrator, you try to transfer the pain of being unable to protect or defend what you feel is rightfully yours. Revenge expunges the emotional stain caused by the humiliation.

Revenge is a fairly specific phenomenon. Tony's fury about being robbed and violated initiated his desire for retaliation – the injury to his sense of himself as a protective father, the hurt he felt for his sons and the rage he felt towards the bullies all came together in a desire to pulverise the 16-year-olds. In defeating them, he felt, he could restore his strength and power.

Fantasies of revenge also arise when a person feels overlooked, misunderstood or disapproved of. Who hasn't been slighted, dismissed or hurt by a teacher, a parent or a stranger and felt, 'I'll show them' in response? We all have the potential to produce vengeful fantasies when we are unfairly treated aggressively, misjudged or taken advantage of. The revenge tries to reverse the feeling of invalidation through a kind of psychological justice: 'I will be validated'; 'You will have to notice me'; or 'You will squirm and hurt as I have had to.' Always, there is a sense that self-respect or self-esteem has been torn from you. There has been a theft, an egregious impropriety, which encourages fantasies of active revenge as an act of assertion that will restore integrity to the lost self.

Embedded into and woven through these themes of spoiling, violation and helplessness is a sense of shocked betrayal. It is almost as if the aggrieved person is forced to recognise something about their own innocence or naïvety. The pain of feeling robbed is often compounded by an accompanying sense of being naïve, an idealist, someone who has not adjusted to how the world really is and is therefore in some way stupid for not having assessed the risks accurately.

In revenge, the recognition that the world can be cruel and unfair is at once rejected and confirmed. One is stunned by betrayal. The act of vengeance tries both to eliminate and to mark that event.

But ultimately, it is the wound of revealed powerlessness that drives our fantasies of revenge. And this outrage – that boundaries have been transgressed – doesn't find expression just in the dramas of private life, but also in the political responses of nations that use retaliation and revenge in their political rhetoric as a means of reassuring the public that their rulers are defending their security. In domestic politics, the wish to 'lock 'em up' or for 'zero tolerance' is a retaliation for the feelings aroused when public safety has been compromised and the social expectation of trust is no longer possible. Instead of thinking about why public space has become increasingly violent and unsafe, the impulse is to exclude, punish and shame those who have despoiled what was once regarded as safe and reliable.

This is not to argue that we need to sanitise our responses in such a way that revenge is expunged from the emotional or social landscape. Such a reaction is a nonsense. But it is worth asking ourselves why, if we try to educate our children out of the belief in 'an eye for an eye' because we consider such an attitude to be an expression of immaturity, we are nevertheless increasingly prepared to indulge that same belief in our legal system and in our political rhetoric.

What do we find so hard to confront? Might it be desperation at realising we are powerless when we had assumed otherwise? Might it be that we experience a version of what is felt by the person or people who inflict the pain on us, and we simply can't bear it? Or might it be that we fail to recognise how overwhelmed we are by disagreeable feelings – so, instead of considering and analysing the complex routes of the aggression coming at us, we furiously send it back in an attempt to negate what has been dumped on us?

Crying Shame

A woman in great distress is unable to stop sobbing. Friends enter the bedroom where she lies to comfort her, to be with her. Their presence increases the flow of her tears. Between wiping her face and heaving, she peers up to see them. She hesitates to meet their gaze: to look at them increases what is already unbearable. She apologises. The exposure of her pain is humiliating. She apologises some more. They shush-shush her. That seems to make things worse. They try to cheer her up. No help. Eventually they sit quietly. She settles. The tears take on a more even flow – until someone else enters the room. Then the cycle restarts. The depression that is being experienced has an added potency because it is witnessed: the potency of shame.

It could be said that therapists deal in shame. It's often what comes along with the person who seeks help. Diffident, tearful, angry, confused, bereaved or hurt, shame is a frequent accompaniment to psychic pain. As therapy has become more socially acceptable (just!), it is caricatured by its detractors and trivialisers as a cosy, indulgent place where people breeze into the consulting room, plonk their problems before their analysts and, Bob's Your Uncle, the interpretative work can begin. But in reality such is seldom the case.

Shame is rarely missing from the beginning of a therapy. It has to be got out of the way, so that the distress that tortures the person can be attended to, as well as needing to be addressed in its own right. Shame is both a shield against other feelings (hurt, anger, despondency) that are uncomfortable as well as an important state of mind.

The Ten Commandments once served as a public standard which if breached could induce personal and community shame. Each culture creates standards for private and public conduct which when violated engender shame. In this context shame is the emotional social conscience. Transgression costs. We aren't supposed to want our ageing parents dead, to envy our friends' fortune, to wish badly on others. These are feelings we are not supposed to have. If we do have such thoughts, shame keeps them tightly bounded in and away from exposure, choking our ability to explore what they mean.

At a more private level, deeply confusing and embarrassing experiences can take on the tint of shame in one's own eyes. The woman who lies crying in her bed doesn't only avert her eyes. She may also search for an acceptance in the eyes of another which is lacking inside herself. She seeks the unjudging gaze which can bear to look, which can receive and tolerate her pain. If she finds this, it helps to dissolve the disgrace and shame. Relieved of the shame, she has a glimmer that her pain can be accepted. She can then experience the main feelings with less conflict because she does not have to feel ashamed that she has such feelings in the first place.

Scorn and ridicule also play their part. When a child shows its interest in something which the adult around feels is inappropriate, the child's interest and desire may go underground. Buried with it may be a sense of shame for having wanted something that was found to be unwelcome. Shameful feelings arise out of a boomerang effect. The child reveals an emotional state which stirs discomfort in the adult; the adult appears to reject the child and what it is feeling and returns the feeling to the child, now encoded with the sense that they were all wrong for feeling or showing it in the first place.

The little boy who cries when his father goes away on a work trip is told that Daddy will be back soon, so there is no need to get upset. This benign comment is not meant to hurt the child. But the child experiences the words not as comforting but as condemnation for what he feels. His feeling of being upset is invalidated. He is now not only upset but misunderstood, and a little embarrassed for feeling upset in the first place. Shame then comes in as a force which both silences and crushes him.

Later on in life, this young man experiences feelings of abandonment when separated from his girl-friend. He is so humiliated by these feelings, so unsure about whether he will be ridiculed if he tells her, that he keeps silent. He acts nonchalant and uncaring. He fears that revealing how he feels will amplify rather than decrease his shame.

It is rarely the child's feelings *per se* that generate shame. Shame is a result of what is stimulated in the adult and then served back to the child as disapproval about its feelings or actions. The little girl who spins around the room, enjoying the way her skirt swirls, can be stopped in her tracks when her uncle, uncomfortable about her knickers showing, admonishes her: 'That's quite enough now, dear.' Her free expression is not only halted, it is given up with an attendant sense of the shame of having done something (but what?) wrong. Shame then inhibits her. As she grows up she is embarrassed about dancing, watchful of herself. The idea of movement becomes linked with shame.

Shame is an internal censor, checking our thoughts and desires, sometimes protecting us from transgression but more habitually constraining desire. Often the desire can't even be examined because it is fused with a shame which acts as a pro-hibition. Shame tells us that it is wrong to want.

But as much as shame relates to childhood humiliation, it is also an indispensable part of social and emotional life. An emo-tional stance which lacks any sense of shame can indicate that a person has difficulty in accepting their hurt as real. Their pain, disconnected and unwarranted, feels more like an inconven-ience that has somehow landed on them: a pain they would be done with – and quickly, please.

The absence of feeling ashamed can indicate that hurt is being expelled in place of being acknowledged. Pain is not something the person is used to bearing. Instead, they are inclined to explode on to others when upset overwhelms them. As they evacuate their pain they refuse responsibility for it. The bystander finds her or himself absorbing what the exploding person couldn't contain.

It is in this sense that shame is a developmental step. When someone can see themself in relation to another instead of viewing the other as the sole cause of their pain, or considering her or himself as the only victim in any given situation, shame has a useful role to play. Shame here shows sensitivity to others and their needs. One feels ashamed because one has acted in a thoughtless way. One would much prefer to have been different. Taking on some responsibility for causing or creating hurt initiates a kind of healing.

This kind of shame, the least toxic and corrosive, can serve as a corrective. Where shame is related to an unflattering exposure of self, it can become a source for self-reflection. Making a mistake and feeling ashamed can be humbling without being devastating. It can have a curative effect, allowing the person to (re)view themself and take stock of their capabilities. Where shame takes over as the main channel to self-experience it becomes disabling. But where it functions for the individual as an early warning system, alerting them to things that cause them degrees of discomfort, it can be useful.

Shame is never absent in any culture. It is a regulator, a source of morality, a set of stories and a standard to live by which a culture creates for itself. The suppression of shame is an alarm signal alerting us to the continual violation of cultural mores, the failure of the culture to meet important needs and the consequent disintegration of interpersonal responsibility.

Hidden Insecurities

How is it that people who are friends can insult one another behind their backs? What need is being served when one joins with another in belittling a friend?

This way of talking has, as I have suggested earlier, the taint of gossip and gossip fulfils many functions. Frequently centred on distant public figures – actors, politicians, royalty – our confusions, our aggression and our longings are flung on to people whose personalities and life experiences we construct in our own terms. Our projections are safe there. We criticise and condemn behaviour that is writ large; we can bond together with perfect strangers over what we abhor or approve. The personalities, our people icons, become the vehicles for creating a sense of an emotional global (or at least a national or Western) village. The gossip coheres a sense of values and a sense of belonging in contexts in which life is often disjointed and disconnected.

Gossip, I have also suggested, helps individuals to articulate, evaluate, clarify or try out their personal feelings and moral systems. In the condemnation or defence of another's behaviour, one is safely venting feelings, while at the same time assessing how one imagines one would act in the same situation. 'Yes, I could imagine myself doing that.' 'No, I cannot fathom doing that.' The gossip has the potential to be a route to self-discovery. We extend the necessarily limited scope of our individual lives by inserting ourselves into the scenarios of another.

So much for the positive aspects. But what is going on when friends put each other down behind their backs, when the gossip is not about people one doesn't know but about people who matter a lot, who are part of one's emotional geography. For some people, talking together about a third person is a prelude to bringing up the difficulties to the person in question. If hurt by one friend, we may talk this through with another in order to clear confusion and so on before engaging the person who hurt us directly. This is a valued aspect of friendship.

But what is happening when the intent is not to understand a hurt but rather to insult, to belittle, to diminish? What is trying to be handled?

Alastair was a composer in quite some demand. His partner Rebecca was a well-regarded radio producer. The face they presented to the world was as a confident couple, perhaps rather wrapped up in each other. It was when they chatted about their friends that a false note was struck. With a mixture of theatrical exuberance and bitchiness, they inevitably described their friends in superlatives – either negative or positive.

Confronted one day by a friend who was offended by the

relish with which the two of them jointly slighted a mutual friend, they were forced to either rubbish her in turn or consider what they were doing. Although they clearly did find pleasure in the routine faulting of colleagues and friends ('he's not very good really, is he?' or 'she may be clever but did you see her hair colour – at her age?'), they were also offended by their behaviour and intrigued as to why it was a compelling way to relate. As a game (because they couldn't at one level bear to take the criticism seriously), they decided to desist from these kinds of pronouncements for a few days. They were startled by the function this extravagant description of their friends contained, unaware of the psychological functions it had served in their relationship and for each of them individually.

Although they were very social, their theatricality disguised the feelings of riskiness which genuine contact with others outside the couple aroused in them. Since nobody else was ever really good enough, and their friends' strengths could be negated by their blubbing witticisms, Alastair and Rebecca could be free of worry about the encroachment or temptations of other relationships.

Though they loved their friends, by demarcating them as 'not quite' or 'a bit too' they protected themselves from what they unknowingly perceived as dangerous. In addition, via their deprecation of others, they temporarily eased their own feelings of inferiority. The diminishing of their friends' attributes thus both bolstered and then helped them deal with their own bad feelings as well as cementing two insecure people together.

The barbed quip which created a distance from others propped up shared insecurities which had brought them together. They had recognised in one another a fragility which craved intense involvement. Part of the contact between them was to shield one another from their fragile feelings by using others to avoid their personal difficulties and enshrining one another and their relationship as sacred.

Behind Alastair's competence was a fierce competitiveness which covered up feelings of inadequacy. Behind Rebecca's confident face to the world lay her envy of others and her unease with her own desires. The way they set up their relationship had ensured that they could protect themselves from these personal difficulties by projecting them out. But refraining from putting down friends enabled both of them to develop insight into their relationship, allowing them to explore what was troubling them individually and how they could help one another more directly.

Their previous solution of exporting their insecurities by elevating themselves above their friends and operating as though in an emotional bunker could be released, freeing them to abandon some of the siege mentality that marked their actions. The insecurities each one had brought into the relationship now became an arena to be addressed rather than to be reinforced. Their genuine interest in others could also be pursued without the bad taste of the backhanded barb, ensuring that the love they had for friends, individually and as a couple, could be allowed to penetrate and warm them rather than be a threatening event.

Betrayal

The word infidelity derives from two ideas. One is related to non-conformity, or altering; the other is related to betrayal. These two very different ideas span the range of views we hold towards sexual liaisons outside a primary (sexually defined) relationship, and they affect how the 'cuckold' is seen, how she or he sees themself, and how they interpret the actions of their adulterous partner.

To some extent, the response of the person whose partner is having an affair will depend upon the state of their relationship and the agreement between them. A woman who has fallen out of love with her man and yet who is pressed to provide sexual services for him may feel relieved when he takes up with someone else. She may also feel nervous about the implications of his sexual activities elsewhere and the threat it poses to their attachment. If the man is reasonably open and they can discuss how the new situation affects their primary relationship over time, then she may be able to live in a relatively secure 'semi-detached' situation where the changes are absorbed and reflected upon.

But this is rarely the case. For many, the outside sexual liaison poses a threat, is meant to pose a threat, or the actions of the adulterer are carried out in such a way that they induce considerable threat.

Malcolm ran into and slept with his ex-lover, Annie, at a conference. They had had a tormented relationship 10 years previously, and since it ended Malcolm had lived happily with Rose. Rose had always felt threatened by Annie because she sensed that for Malcolm there was something in the ending of that relationship which was not quite complete, but Malcolm had reassured her of his commitment and eventually her jealousy dissipated. Out of the blue, from Rose's perspective, a long, long letter arrived from Annie which Malcolm read, threw away and would not comment on. He then moved guiltily around Rose for the next few weeks and when she would try to ask him about the letter he would respond as though affronted by saying, 'I didn't do anything to provoke it. It had nothing to do with me.' He would then withdraw. There was no space for Rose or Malcolm to say how the letter affected them and Rose was left with feelings of exclusion and the question as to why the letter had suddenly appeared.

Malcolm's response to the letter and to his infidelity had an important impact on Rose. She felt that she must be imagining things, that she had transgressed on his privacy (after all, it wasn't his fault Annie had written to him), and that she had a problem with her feelings of insecurity. She blamed herself for the bad feelings between them and worked hard on herself to overcome her unfounded jealousy.

This set-up, in which the actions of the adulterer are concealed, creates a situation in which the person who has been betrayed has no test of reality and can feel quite mad. I use the word betrayed, because they had a monogamous contract between the two of them. Malcolm's infidelity towards Rose and the knock-on letter stirred up a rash of feelings that he was unable to handle except through guilt and withdrawal. Denying his part in the letter left Rose responsible for all the weird things that were going on between them. Malcolm felt that in sleeping with Annie he had betrayed Rose but he hadn't betrayed himself. He hadn't sorted out the way in which it had felt right for him to sleep with Annie, and how that was to do with the past. He himself was annoyed by the letter because he felt that Annie had misconstrued his actions.

When the background to the letter came out two years later, Rose felt that she had not been betrayed by Malcolm's sleeping with Annie (although she hated the thought of it) so much as by his withdrawal and the shifting on to her of all the crazy feelings that had surfaced which she hadn't instigated.

Janine, who was in a monogamous relationship with Heather, slept with Sue. When Heather found out she felt extremely threatened and didn't feel able to continue the relationship. Although Heather and Janine had a good relationship which Janine wanted to continue, Heather felt dirtied by what had happened. She felt Janine's apologies and explanations were a way for Janine to let herself off the hook. A basic trust had been broken. There was, she felt, something sacrosanct about the physical relationship between them. It had touched her deeper than language could express and her rejection of Janine was almost involuntary. She would try to forgive, but she couldn't forget.

For a long time, it felt to her as though her body refused to be open. She could go through the motions of lovemaking; she could tell herself that she was punishing both of them unnecessarily; she could tell herself to stop being a victim, but the block existed. Fortunately Janine could see the effect of her actions, and accepted the hurt she caused, but also insisted that she was there for Heather. After some time, Heather realised that she'd rebuilt her trust and became less fearful; she realised that she did not produce images of victimisation whenever they were close. They had worked through the dislocation in their relationship together.

For all who are susceptible to it, the feelings of jealousy are excruciating and almost physically uncontainable. Conventional wisdom says that when the man is able to re-assert his sexual ownership or mastery over his woman by sleeping with her again, he can discharge his discomfort. But this is too insensitive to men's equally excruciating feelings of jealousy. It denies men's expressiveness and sees their sexuality as simply a weapon rather than their emotional humanity.

Betrayal hurts. It is an attack on a belief system, and can force the betrayed to question the basis of what they rely upon. To be sexually betrayed may make one rethink what is to be believed and trusted. It is not simply the betrayer who is distrusted and castigated. Until the experience can be integrated, jealousy and guilt are the hallmark responses. Betrayal does mark a change, it is a watershed in relation to the self and others. The emotional aftershocks reverberate alongside the hurt and confusion; when it all stills, the process of repositioning and reappraisal occurs. Assumptions and expectations are reformulated, which may make for a more authentic basis from which to relate.

Disappointment

The paucity of language we have to describe emotional life can constrain our capacity to communicate the range and subtlety of our emotional responses. We then organise our emotional lives under the umbrella of the grand passions – love, hate, envy, lust, anger, grief and jealousy. But in so doing, emotional responses which are more subtle – but equally compelling, affecting and decisive in the life of the individual – can be lost, skirted over, insufficiently understood and explored.

Such is the case with the emotional and psychological state of disappointment. In fact, in a paradoxical play of our uptightness and inarticulateness around emotional expression, the thin-lipped utterance 'I'm disappointed' is a damning indictment, a code word for anger or disapproval, the signal for closure of the conversation.

Today, with the consensus that a wider range of emotional expressions is beneficial, it is useful to cast an eye on disappointment once again; to understand why it can often be hard to assimilate emotionally, and what happens when it cannot be recognised. For example, where does it go? What does it turn into? What defences are brought into play for displacing disappointment when it can't be acknowledged?

If one's emotional muscles have been trained to allow one to experience disappointment, then it will be known as a feeling associated with hope or expectations gone wrong and the hurt of let-down. Disappointment experienced in this straightforward way allows the thwarting of promise to be lamented.

Often the closest we come to acknowledging the depth of feeling generated by disappointment is when it is linked with the word bitter. 'Bitter disappointment' conveys the searing hurt of an entirely reasonable expectation being destroyed. The bitterness suggests a sense of wizening and contracting; the organism receives a blow and folds into itself. As the acrid taste permeates one's senses, disappointment is assimilated. The intensity of bitter disappointment is as powerful as any of the grand passions.

In time the blow heals. The emotional passage through disappointment starts with a shock, which then gives way to feelings of hurt and injury. From that may follow questioning, confusion and anger until the recognition of promise defeated is absorbed. This sequence is one of many possible ways of coming to terms with disappointment.

Disappointment contains within it a diversity of affective responses which, if experienced, allow the disappointment to be felt fully and then to be done with. But if the individual has no emotional place to register his or her encounters with disappointment because they have been consistently mislabelled and diverted elsewhere, when disappointment occurs it will be harder for it to be experienced in all its subtlety. It will become instead an emotionally troublesome state that has to be shunted off elsewhere, processed through the psychic pathways that are well worn in that individual.

Those psychic pathways have to convert the feeling states associated with disappointment into emotions it can recognise. Most commonly, disappointment which is unable to be experienced directly finds new life as anger. Anger then becomes the expulsive expression of disappointment that can't be felt and assimilated.

Once transformed into anger, disappointment has to be expunged: it is acted upon and flung outside the person rather than held and contained. The expulsive anger disturbs the interpersonal field around the individual and it may cause confusion to those caught in its expression, for it seems to have no basis. In addition, it can feel dangerous both to the expellee as well as to others, because it feels unmotivated or entirely inappropriate.

Because the anger is a substitute for disappointment, its discharge provides only temporary relief. The anger is unsatisfying; its inauthenticity makes it an inaccurate vehicle. It swerves around looking for a parking place but, vaguely out of control, it can't easily come to rest and revs itself up as though looking for trouble.

Such uncorked anger as a substitute for disappointment contains meanings which can usefully be thought of as the germ of the psyche's attempt to stand up for itself. In order to receive, digest and assimilate disappointment, the psyche must embody a self capable of sustaining a range of emotional responses. But when our range of emotional responses has been clipped, the result is a diminution of the sense of self. The diverted emotions that can't be felt get converted, exported, split off or disregarded in one way or another. Their separation within the psyche into different compartments or away from the central experience of self leads to a reduced sense of self. This experience is akin to a private emotional assault on the person, who then asserts his or her anger.

As they occupy this emotion, they take up a physical/mental space that counteracts the sense of being diminished. For a short period, the emotional space they inhabit satisfies the divided self.

Disappointment, on the other hand, implies the capacity to mourn and accept loss without feeling shamed by the frustrated desire which has not been met.

Many are unable to face or feel disappointment because the longings and hopes behind it are experienced as so problematic and shameful. Desire arises side by side with conflict, and it is this unentitlement to desire that forms a precursor to the difficulty experienced in feeling disappointment. Without the capacity to want freely, it is hard to experience disappointment.

Although we may not yet have receptors to meet certain feelings because we slot them into alternative emotional pigeon-holes, we can expand our emotional literacy by using words that more accurately describe the scope and variety of our experiences.

When we are able to find an authentic language with which to express our feelings, we extend our experience of self. We then hold the complexity of our feelings within our own person, where we have the choice to act on them rather than be pushed into expelling them.

SECTION II

Public Life

Public Emotions and Political Literacy

The year 1998 saw public emotions appear in unusual and unexpected arenas. We've had emotional militancy over Louise Woodward, individual football players, Mary Bell and suspected paedophiles in ways which are confusing and sometimes alarming reminiscent of a mob.

A mob is by definition fickle. It lacks political nous or political sophistication and it is always dominated and motivated by emotional considerations. That's what distinguishes it from a political protest or political expression. The aroused mob is a counterpoint to the depoliticising of our culture; a predictable response to a kind of ennui or a sense of hopelessness in which political participation seems impossible or ineffective. When it's hard to feel politically effective or even visible, a way to be seen (if not heard) and to make common cause is to make a protest of an emotional nature. It renders a different kind of authenticity and punches with a different kind of power.

It's not that emotions have no place in political and public life. They do, and they are central to any revitalisation of public life. Many of our most important economic and political decisions are argued over in emotional terms. It's hard to hear the salient political factors in the Europe and Euro debate or the constitutional reforms within Britain itself discussed in political terms. So great is the emotional character of the discourse that the political discussion (such as it is) is framed by politicians and journalists in emotional terms. Issues of national identity, of Britain's place in the world, of the political alliances it might be making are silenced under emotive language which still sets the political discussion in terms of 'them and us' and avoids the real political issues which Britain needs to come to terms with economically and socially.

Emotions are right at the centre of individuals' private lives and the nation's public life, but at present they are there in a way that degrades the political process and political participation. The recent mass demonstrations of feelings are not an unambiguous victory for those struggling to put emotional literacy on the agenda. On the contrary. Such demonstrations indicate rather how squeezed our political responses have become on the one hand, and the paucity of opportunity we have for the digestion and expression of emotional issues such as grief, anger, helplessness, on the other.

The reason why some politicians have supported Antidote – the organisation committed to bringing emotional literacy to public and private life – is not because they want more raw emotions in public life, or counselling in the House of

Commons or trauma therapy instead of programmes to alleviate poverty, but because they recognise only too well how many of our presumed political decisions are played as emotional decisions (such as Europe) and how many of our emotional decisions (such as racism) require political and economic response. They want to change this.

They recognise too that an adversarial political system is not the most enlightened way to move thinking, or society, forward; that deeper, more complex ways of thinking are required; that some of our most fundamental political acts have enormous emotional implications on people's lives, and that we need to include them when considering legislation. They also recognise that fear, blame, shame are the emotional tools politicians use to temporarily circumvent tricky political, economic and social problems.

Other politicians are more cynical. They dip into our emotional lives as though they were a pool of pure response which they can analyse to see how to present what they wish to do. They use polling to see how the public might feel about an intended policy and how then to present it in its most palatable form. The energy goes into presentation rather than getting the policy as right as possible. This kind of polling is hardly the translation of emotional literacy into public life. It's more akin to advertising. If we present the material this way, will they buy it? No, let's try it this way. Oops, that doesn't work either. Let's hear what the objections are so we can refine how we present it.

Today, politicians poll to control, not to assess what people want. Citizens' juries or 'unfocus' groups in which people are able to talk in open-ended ways about how policy initiatives might work are a long way from the knee-jerk emotionalism of

the pollster who sets up the calls to work out how to sell the
policy, not whether or not to float it.

Public emotions are not necessarily an expression of emotional literacy at all. They frequently are the very opposite; the
result of the difficulty we have accepting in our individual and
collective emotional responses to what is before us privately
and publicly. Emotional literacy means being able to recognise
what you are feeling so that it doesn't interfere with thinking. It
becomes another dimension to draw upon when making decisions or on encountering situations. Emotional expression, by
contrast, can mean being driven by emotions so that it isn't
possible to think. These two things are often confused because
we are still uncomfortable with the idea of the validity of feelings. We allow them in certain kinds of endeavours and exempt
them in others.

We are not a football-crazy world because football really is
the most important thing, but because the emotional states and
political issues it is able to carry provide one of the few
mechanisms of shared expression that we have today. Football-
watching is the collective celebration of human skills. For the
most part our shared experiences come from the marketplace
through buying branded goods rather than creating, agreeing,
enjoying things together. Football not only embraces many different things collectively, but is meaningful because it carries
emotional responses which both belong to it and don't belong
to it and which aren't as easily expressed elsewhere – feelings of
winning and losing, of being let down, of hurting, of being
furious, of being ecstatic.

Even when public emotions seem to present something we
might welcome such as the feelings of relief felt after the

General Election, or the challenge to the National Front in France which the world cup victory implied, we might want to reflect more deeply on what Decca Aitkenhead has called the post-ideological culture. For emotions abstracted, exploited or promoted are surely no substitute for the kind of rigorous political and strategic thinking required to understand our world and the difficulties it presents to us. There is a real difference between bringing emotional literacy *to* the political agenda and substituting emotions *for* a political agenda. There is a real difference too between bringing personal issues into the political framework – relationships, work and home, parents and children – and understanding the political nature of such relations versus the elevation of the columnist/personal story as the way in which the personal is considered.

Everywhere we witness the depoliticisation of our culture. Rather than deepening the political by linking what people feel and the conflicts we need to come to terms with, we strip the emotional of its connection to the political. Emotional literacy by contrast increases political literacy by joining issues where they need to be joined and separating political and emotional issues when they have become fused. It's not a substitute for political expression but a strengthening of it.

Hysteria Politics

Is this really the best we can do? Is chasing Mary Bell or hounding convicted paedophiles the way in which we as a society want to come to terms with what people find abhorrent? Is focusing on the fact or the alleged size of Bell's payment from Gitta Sereny of any kind of relevance? Is our political leadership really so unable to do more than chase the rear by attacking Mary Bell for financially profiting from her crimes?

In the absence of an exploration of the fear, horror and disturbance that paedophilia or Mary Bell's acts of killing when she was ten arouse, we find ourselves in the midst of hysteria politics in which the modern equivalent of the lynch mob (stimulated by the tabloid papers and the talk shows) becomes not an expression of our humanity but – in its enactment of hate and censure – a terrifying version of the evil that has been projected on to Mary Bell and the child abusers.

It's easy to hate and to exclude. Our century is filled with the mobilisation of hate to exclude one group or another. The wars we remember as heroic and the wars we regard as misguided or immoral depend upon the casting of one group – racial, ethnic, national – as the enemy; the *reason* why things aren't right. And yet we know it isn't so. We know that the making of enemies is a mechanism by which we put outside of ourselves anything which we find unpalatable or difficult, and erect a *cordon sanitaire* around it. By finding an external enemy we think we can excise what is so troublesome.

If we look more deeply at the psychological processes set in train inside us when something as troublesome as the issues surrounding paedophilia or a child who murdered are aroused, we might find more creative ways to respond. We might be able to clear the space to think about such horrors rather than hound the perpetrators as though that were some kind of solution.

There is no way that a parent will not feel fearful when hearing that an active paedophile is in the neighbourhood. Accompanying the fear, the parent has to confront unexpected feelings of powerlessness, of recognising that they may be unable to offer their child safety and protection not just from this paedophile but from the sexual intrusions of others. Issues hitherto at the back of one's mind come to the forefront, and the world can feel very unsafe for parents in this situation.

It would be a strange person who didn't feel diminished by such feelings. It is as though one's sense of confidence about what one can provide as a parent has been stolen. One goes from feeling threatened to finding oneself angry or dejected. We then seek to punish those who make us feel this way. When fear intersects with (or induces feelings of) powerlessness, it's a potent cocktail for any individual, and the impulse to try to expel these feelings on to something or someone or some other group is almost unavoidable.

The individual may gather a temporary sense of strength from attacking the perpetrator of their terror. This makes a lot of psychological sense in the short term, for it is how we can respond initially. But after the initial impulse, if we continue to express our fear and respond to our feelings of powerlessness in this way, we've solved nothing. We've simply put the feelings outside ourselves, transformed them into something else which needs constant reinforcing to ensure only a tenuous recovery of our feelings of safety. Politically, it doesn't make a whole lot of sense, however. Routing our enemies and confining them is no basis for a stable society. Indeed, if the information we have about Mary Bell is accurate, she appears to have gone from one nightmare life with her mother into a care situation in which she was sexually exploited, rather than helped.

Disturbed children and disturbed adults trouble and alarm us. There is no way they won't and can't. Their responses to the situations they have encountered are reproduced in terms similar to or emotionally congruent with those in which they first experienced their disturbance.

We need to take heed of how the disturbances of others affect us. In the case of the treatment of sexual offenders or children who murder, our responses are a clue to the mess we are in. Our desire to silence them has an equivalent in the very acts we deplore from them. We want to block out something just as, in their disregard and exploitation of the other, the child sex molester or the child murderer has wanted to silence the needs of the other. The difficulty is that children and adults who murder and hurt children do not do so from the perspective of absolute cruelty. It is far more complex than this. They don't set out to pervert relationship, it is more that the relationships they have been exposed to, which have salience for them, are marked by cruelty, abuse, neglect and exploitation. This becomes a template for relationship and cannot be deconstructed and reconstructed without enormous work.

This is not to say that we don't need to take action to protect ourselves and our children from people who have so been treated. Of course that is an essential first step. Political leadership means showing people that one understands their fears and their concerns. Those cannot be denied. But we need then to build from there, to talk about what we can best do to face up to the horror in our midst. The attack on released convicted paedophiles and on Mary Bell carry within them agendas about society spinning out of control.

A sensitive leadership could address the issues surrounding children's needs and our wish to protect them and link these with current initiatives which go against the exploitation of children. And it could go further. It could explain how the tendency each individual and each group in a society has to want to separate itself off from what we find abhorrent by designating it outside of ourselves, is the way a society goes on auto-destruct.

Our political leadership could reverse the damage of previous thoughtless statements by demonstrating that in this important time, as the Government is trying to remake our society, we have a responsibility through our institutions – the school, the family, work, welfare and health – to find ways not of splitting

off what we find horrific but of finding ways to transform the
conditions that create it. This would reduce the panic that has
been aroused and begin the process whereby we all feel
included, both those who fear harm and those who have been
so harmed that they have harmed others.

When Truth is not Enough

A t a demonstration outside South Africa House following the killing of Ruth First in 1982, I was struck by the command of the chant 'Don't mourn, mobilise'. Could that be correct? Was it right to express outrage for the assassination of one of the heroes of the struggle for South Africa by condemning or sidelining mourning? To be sure, more deaths lay ahead but why the taboo on mourning? What was the fear behind it: that the movement would succumb to tears and be able to fight no longer?

The chant was easy enough to change, to move from a negative to the imperative 'Mourn and mobilise'. Leaving space to consider loss rather than deny it seemed a not unreasonable condition to expect from a political movement aiming to create a new society.

What underpins the rationale of the Truth Commissions in

South Africa and Bosnia is a sense that for a society to move on, for it to reconcile, for any kind of new social contact to be forged, the past has to be faced. A truth, the truth has to be exposed. It has to be discussed, it has to be confronted, the terrible hurt and losses incurred and still felt have to be made visible and the nefarious deeds carried out by individuals and agencies of state have to be laid bare in front of the nation.

There are many truths that need facing and as the South African Truth and Reconciliation Commission says in response to statements lodged with it, much pain that needs to be acknowledged. It thanks those who have submitted evidence to it with 'entrusting the memories of what happened to you in the past', going on to state 'You have made known to us what you had to endure over the years . . . your statement will help to establish the truth about our past and assist in achieving the healing you and our country needs.'

But, as Michael Ignatieff has asked in *Index on Censorship*, are nations really like people who have memories and traumas that, once confronted, can be reconciled? Truth Commissions, he argues, can change the nature of public discussion by forcing into public awareness testimony and memory which have been excluded or denied. They can insist that the history of a country includes fuller accounts of the deeds of the oppressors and the costs of those deeds, but he is quite correct in suggesting that we cannot equate the psyche of societies and nations with that of individuals. Neither can we see the work of a Truth Commission as simply a public version of the private therapy a traumatised individual may undergo.

As Gillian Slovo's film *Death in the Family* shows, finding and confronting those who actually killed her mother, Ruth First, is an important part of her continuing attempts to come to terms with her death. But of course the concept of coming to terms with is too static. By its very nature a trauma can never be satisfactorily worked through: that is an idealised understanding of what it means to put one's history in the past. Rather, a trauma's consequences are ubiquitous and labile. They can certainly be modified but they emerge time and again forcing the individual to re-engage.

There is no one single understanding that truth allows. To know what happened and how; to be able to give an account of one's pain as the South African Truth Commission invites; to be heard in a public forum where private agony caused by an unrecognised war is now set in context is undoubtedly important; to be able to grieve publicly and privately rather than have one's desire to mourn derided; for a society to have its pain about injustice registered; all such developments are crucial and they are part of a process of reconciliation or forgiveness.

But truth, essential as it is, cannot stem the tide of distress. It can be enormously helpful to have one's truth acknowledged and to learn the details of what occurred. It can often be important for a survivor to confront a perpetrator with his or her own actions. The perpetrator has stolen something precious from the person and although whatever has been taken cannot be given back, the feeling of continuing helplessness or victimisation can be transformed. In a successful encounter, what changes is that one is no longer vulnerable to the perpetrators. They can't take anything else away. What is restored is the emotional strength and dignity that were stolen by the perpetrator. In a public encounter, others bear witness and by their witness temporarily share the pain and show their support.

A Truth Commission can legitimate the wounds the individual and the nation carries, it can try to address what the survivor requires of it (for example the South African Truth Commission asks what action the litigant would like taken). It can make part of public consciousness the real and continuing cost of apartheid to individuals and to the society, it can underpin the need to mourn, to insist that individual perpetrators face the impact of their actions, it can reshape the historical account. Publicly encouraged and sanctioned speaking out moves from the margins, to become a central issue, the emotional consequences of political action. But just as trauma caused by abuse is different from the trauma of the death of a sibling or a parent in childhood, so is the trauma that results from political repression. A parent losing a child to an early death because of illness faces a different loss from that of a parent of one of Argentina's disappeared. The way the parent experiences the loss and lives with it subsequently, takes its complexion from the explanations they provide for themselves about the loss. Their anger, sadness, grief, despair, embody the particulars of their circumstances as well as reflect their individual psychologies.

Fifty years on the Holocaust has taught us that loss and trauma are not things to which we become easily reconciled. Rather loss and trauma live on, not just in the first generation but in subsequent generations. There is a need to mourn, to grieve, to rage, to go over the events repeatedly as with any trauma. To conceal the loss or trauma, as so many Central European Jewish refugees had to, unwittingly exacerbates the wound. Undoubtedly the Truth Commission facilitates the public and therefore the private and personal recognition of the many traumas experienced in South Africa's recent past.

Understanding the damage caused in other societies by a denial of the past the Truth Commission refuses to hide the many outrages, atrocities and wounds in South Africa's history in the vain hope that without a reckoning, normal life will just carry on. The Truth Commission is crucial to and perhaps will be decisive in making the new South Africa. But as the Truth Commission openly acknowledges, it would be equally naïve to think that it can wipe away the emotional pain of the individuals whose lives have been marked by the acts perpetrated under apartheid. Those wounds never completely heal. They create emotional scars which bend the individual's approach to life in ways that reflect the injuries. The trauma is never fully in the past but lives on in the present. Perhaps the most we can hope for is that if the wrongdoing and trauma are allowed to be alive in the present, future generations will experience the repercussions as their history, rather than their present.

Facing Our Fears

My friend lives next door to a family of low-level drug dealers. From eleven o'clock of a morning, young men and a few young women – affecting a look between cool and shifty – intermittently sidle up to the patch in front of the house where, in plain view, money is exchanged for glassine envelopes. As the day wears on, the front patch turns into a hangout and the noise level builds. The little children in the family cry, the music gets turned up and my friend, who works from home, becomes increasingly irritated.

Because she has done some soft drugs in her time, my friend also understands the atmosphere and tries to silence her irritation: 'stop being so middle class and uptight', she counsels herself. By evening there is more disruption. Windows are broken, kids are yelling, what look like stolen radios are being passed in and out of the house.

The police are called. They come, they watch; they talk to the
neighbours, who have magicked away the contraband. For a few
days a police presence on the street ensures some quiet. Trained
to soothe irate middle-class citizens, the police temporarily ease
my friend's distress and they soon fall into discussing the social
despair that causes such careless, criminal and loutish behaviour.
They part muttering Tony Blair's phrase, 'tough on crime,
tough on the causes of crime'.

They both feel helpless.

On my street, a seven-year-old toughie and his two mates of
six and nine bash up the wooden gates and the street signs, and
dismember the hoses and bikes in the front gardens. Hard lads,
not yet in double digits, are practising intimidation. Indifferent
to adult authority, they seem impervious. I go to the parents of
both families, talk with them about what we can do to help the
children on the block to co-operate. Simple scapegoating of
one family is tried, but it doesn't really add up. We are working
on a solution, but we're not there.

Of course, it would be so much more pleasant if the social
tensions being expressed in such nascent banditry could be
made to go away; if a strong anti-crime line, new laws for neigh-
bourliness and a dose of community policing could create the
peaceful, harmonious neighbourhoods of our dreams.

But we are encountering something we have not faced
before. There is now a profound level of social disintegration
and we lack a consensus about how we should live our lives.
This new situation can perplex us intellectually and swamp us
with emotions we neither comprehend nor know how to
process.

Fear, anxiety, anger and helplessness characterise many of

our responses to daily life. We don't like feeling this way. Fearful of engulfment, we discover that we have gravitated towards sets of ideas which at heart we don't really believe in but which temporarily serve as a clamp on our difficult feelings and convert our helplessness, anxiety, anger and fear into the opposite: toughness.

And what of the feckless, marauding youth who are running riot? What motivates their actions, their violence, their destructiveness and social insolence? What does their toughness conceal? Does their bravado cover its opposite: the helplessness, the uselessness, the lack of place which consumer society creates in those who neither produce or consume? In their acts of violence and destruction, are they refusing the place of helplessness which we ask them to inhabit?

If underclass youth is destructive because it is helpless, couldn't it be said that when we are helpless we also become destructive? We become drawn to isolating certain groups and seeing them as 'The Problem'. Wanting to hold our complex feelings of helplessness at bay, we avoid thinking into the complex of issues which are causing such despair, destructiveness and malaise in Britain today, preferring to think into a narrow sphere instead.

In fact, we need to take on these difficult feelings, not shunt them off somewhere less troublesome. Engaging with feelings doesn't prevent thinking; on the contrary, it allows it. Bypassing difficult feelings requires our mental processes to be employed in denial or repression. If we can't confront what is going on, our solutions will seek a cleavage from our experience and drift over into scapegoating, fundamentalism, authoritarianism, vigilantism or nostalgia – responses that reinforce our feelings of helplessness rather than resolving them, which bear the haunting mark of desperation and insolubility.

Desperation, anger and hopelessness are some of the emotional states which right-wing politicians have relied upon and exploited in their quest to underpin authoritarian policies. Such appeals side-step – rather than help us to confront – our present social and economic difficulties. They reflect the desperation of politicians.

When I go round the country, to talk with a wide variety of people about emotional literacy and mental health, I find that once the despair, pessimism and helplessness which has insinuated itself into all our psyches is aired, rather than exploited, the talk turns energetically to politics, to people's daily experiences of life and the wish to influence the political process in new and different ways. Parents, young people, educators, senior police officers, managers, doctors and sportsfolk contribute ideas about how a fresh morality can be created, how our society can be made to work anew.

People are seeking to reverse the moral decline of the last decade. The social movements around animal rights and the environment encode within them a morality missing in conventional politics. They are then often criticised for being emotional movements, movements of the heart rather than the head. Such criticisms are worth deconstructing. They are designed to undercut, to say that the movements are immature, well-meaning, but really hopelessly wrong-headed. The thrust of the attack is to ridicule not just the movements but what motivates them. Feelings as part of politics are just too dangerous!

In the debate about how we can reconstruct our society, create anew a consensus which can contain diversity rather than rely on exclusion, we need to address our fears and not side-step them. We often experience two sets of reactions to our feelings when we confront social disintegration. One is 'lock 'em up' (but for how long and what do we do when they come out?). The other, more thoughtful and complex, includes more questioning: the whys and wherefores of how we've come to be in this situation; the whys and wherefores of how we might reverse decline. This is where the project of emotional literacy comes into play. The counter to fear, to disintegration, to helplessness, is not toughness alone. Engaging with our emotional responses will produce programmes which are more thought through and sophisticated, which don't rely on isolating various groupings as 'the baddies' but allow our energy to think into more comprehensive, inclusive policies. Moral consensus, boundaries, rules, a sense of belonging and of being worthy cannot be imposed, except fleetingly. Belonging, contributing, participating usefully arise when human beings are supported, nurtured and treasured; this starts with our earliest environments. If (as Tony Blair has said) our task now is nothing less than a national renewal, that renewal needs our widest, bravest thinking. Facing our fears rather than papering over them frees up imaginative thinking. We can't manage on less.

The Meaning of Money

No one relishes paying tax. But do we really hate it so much? Do we really want politics reduced to a competition about which party can set a lower rate? If so, why? What does taxation and the Budget mean to us? Are we so alienated from the political process and fiscal policy that we feel the best we can do is find ways to minimise our own liability?

The two major parties are constantly locked into a very narrow argument over how much they will redistribute the tax collected and which interests will be favoured. When a proposed Labour policy is mentioned, every commentator and politician jumps in to question how it is to be funded. But as long as Labour bends over backwards to convince us it isn't going to spend more than the Tories, that it intends to find the money through hyper-efficient management, Labour misses an opportunity to engage people politically and psychologically, and to make the fundamental point that taxation and spending are a particular way of making a contribution to a society and belonging to it. Indeed, part of the appeal of the Liberal Democrats' proposal to put 1p on taxation for education was that it went beyond the pragmatic, the ethical and the just. It reintroduced the notion that the public purse could be a means of social participation.

If the only way in which budgetary changes affect people (whether in or out of paid employment) is in their personal spending, then taxation becomes merely a burden or, for some, a moral obligation. Right-wing parties put forward the argument that low taxation means more personal freedom, and accuse the left of still being silly enough to want to tax and spend. But these responses miss three crucial dimensions: first, that the economy is a social relationship in which we all participate; second, that what now counts as an economic activity is restricted to earners, whereas, as we all know, many activities – raising children, looking after relatives, working in a voluntary capacity, subsistence farming – are economic activities too; third, that we have an emotional relationship to money: it carries meanings for us beyond the literal.

In its 1996 Budget statement, Antidote, then a new organisation committed to bringing psychotherapeutic insights into the public domain, tried to open up the habitual conversations we have about Budgets. Drawing on discussions with a range of people about what money means to them, it noted the emotional costs of the money economy, the perverse way in which the market – the most potent idea in economic practice – creates or compounds feelings of insecurity which it then purports to satisfy. It looked at how money is woven into our sense of self and permeates our relations with one another. This idea is one that, for the most part, we take for granted. We don't question how certain factors affect our individual and collective psychologies: the having of money, or not; the hope that we will have it; the sense that no sum is sufficient to guarantee well-being; the rage or sense of shame that arises from not having money; a loathing of inequality which stains all of our hearts and the fear of the future that hides a difficulty in coming to terms with the precariousness of the present.

We need to understand these effects in some detail before we can dismantle the appeal of the freedom-of-choice-to-spend argument that supposedly accompanies low direct taxation. We don't yet really understand from where the compelling link between freedom and money arises (apart from the drudgery of repetitive, boring and unrecognised work). Freedom from what? Freedom for what? In imagining winning the Lottery, most people will say it buys freedom, but they can't go much further than that. Antidote's research shows that money has become a thing, imbued with all sorts of meanings. We have a relationship *to* money, rather than one that sees money as an expression of a relationship.

As Antidote pointed out, we do not question the assumptions about human nature that underlie our economic theories. So ingrained are the opposing notions of greed and altruism that their bases remain unexplored. In reality these two poles, created within a market economy, are related to each other. Responses that exist inside all of us, they exemplify different aspects of our social and psychological structure.

Nor do we look at the emotional consequences of emotional decisions by making an economic audit. We know, for example, that making an economic investment in emotional literacy pro-grammes – parenting classes, the probation service, schooling, nursery care – can reduce emotional distress for both children and adults (which, if unchecked, ends in greater social upheaval and serious subsequent costs). But these minimal costs at the front end of life are not factored into budgetary decisions. Our Budgets are short-term fixes rather than the expression of a society thinking about itself and auditing its needs.

Money isn't the only thing that makes the world go round, but we act as though it were. To see taxation as a social relation-ship, as a way to contribute to society rather than as something to avoid, we need to be bold. We need to engage with the work of those who challenge our fundamental beliefs about our eco-nomic arrangements, such as the New Economic Foundation, the environmentally-oriented think-tank, and the Letts initia-tives, where a barter system operates. Marilyn Waring, the New Zealand MP-turned-economist, points out that the United Nations' System of National Accounts, which is based on the exchange of money, excludes from economic activity most female, domestic and child-rearing labour, as well as subsistence economies. Furthermore, by employing an accounting system in which economic growth depends upon trade but not its conse-quences – so that selling arms, for example, is reckoned as growth, as is the cost of clearing up the damage from the deploy-ment of those armaments – economic growth actually comes to mean its very opposite in terms of human development.

As long as we exclude unpaid work as economically irrelevant, we are failing to recognise the way in which we are all economic participants. By failing to value people's contributions unless these are expressed monetarily, we collude in making a fetish of money. The emotional and economic costs of this are serious.

After many years of political bullying, a malaise can set in. Political thinking can become uncreative, a response to what *is*, rather than an imaginative endeavour. Budget time gives us a great opportunity to rethink the meanings and centrality of money, the economy, democracy. Daring to think new thoughts about how to value people's work, both paid and unpaid, daring to explore our emotional relationship to money, daring to recognise the emotional costs of fiscal policies; and daring to challenge the received notion of growth – these are places to start. An alternative budget that takes into account the social wealth to which so many people contribute would open a door to participation and a longed-for social consensus. We know that what we have isn't working. Can we dare to think and do differently?

Leading Questions

We are confused about leadership. We can't quite decide whether we like it, whether we think it's a good idea, whether we want it to be strong or more informal, or whether we just prefer to knock it. When leaders appear awkward, we take pot-shots at them rather than use the moment to try to understand what we expect, what we want and what we require.

William Hague's attempts to bond with his colleagues have been much ridiculed, and his leadership style has been contrasted with those of his two recent predecessors; one who was considered weak, the other strong and bullying. Hague is portrayed as someone who hasn't quite grasped what leadership is about. Meanwhile, some Labour MPs are worried about a code of practice that seems to limit their individual initiative.

Lately, we've been hearing that leadership is all. Good leadership, it is often said, is what schools need. Yes, we concur unthinkingly, of course. And when we do think about it, it's obviously right. Dynamic leadership that recognises individual and collective strengths, pushes for excellence, has a 'can-do' attitude to solving problems and is capable of building a team that works well together undoubtedly makes a big difference to any school.

But is leadership becoming a substitute for understanding the intricacies of all sorts of relationships at work, in government and in the community? Has the notion of leadership come to cover so much that the differences between power, authority and effectiveness aren't much thought about? Instead, we couple those words to styles of leadership, as though leadership itself is a given, not an outcome of a situation.

To be sure, some strive to become leaders, but many others who find themselves in leadership positions may not have chosen to be there. They have a certain initiative, which then flourishes so that they find themselves directing a group of staff without much thought about the process of leadership. Then, too, there are those who are promoted from what they are especially good at – teaching, writing or working in a lab – into management, in order to direct a project. They may have the authority that comes from being able and well-respected, but be lacking in leadership skills. They find themselves suddenly in charge, not arguing for their view-point but having it accepted by virtue of their position. Their wishes are now put into practice, whereas the previous month they were not. Now they are looked to for direction, for approval and for recognition from those who were formerly their peers.

This transfer from being one of a group to being its leader

implies a change for all. Often unanticipated are the psychological duties that accompany leadership and the psychological
states that are evoked by others towards those in leadership
positions. Whether it is in a small office, a household, an activity group or a government, people have unvoiced and often
unrecognised expectations of their leaders. Leaders become
imbued with the capacity to make things all right – things that
they have no ability to make right as well as those which they
can influence. Carrying the buck means carrying people's
unconscious expectations; it also means being prone to disap-
point them at any moment for something one isn't even aware
of. Leaders can be expected to work miracles, to help their
group face difficult issues, inspire and protect.

Almost everyone wants to be quietly recognised for their
capabilities and encouraged to express their best. An individual
with a history of not being supported may create havoc within
a group – or for the leader. The leader may feel that he or she is
being asked to make up for a deficit in the past. This isn't made
any easier by the fact that neither the person looking for reassurance nor the leader being asked for it is especially aware that
these processes are taking place. Instead, an incomprehensible
undercurrent of attack or disappointment that is hard to address
may undermine the harmony of the group.

It's no wonder, then, that one requirement of leadership is
the capacity to handle criticism; not so much to withstand and
endure it, but to be able to distil the essence of it so that it can
be examined and responded to. Many people's leadership falters
at this point because the weight of unsolicited projections trans-
ferred on to them can feel like an assault – undeserved and
uncalled for. They can either become brusque and bullying to

protect themselves, or they can create a wall against hearing criticism. Those who do find a way to absorb it, to feel the hurt that can go along with an unprovoked attack and then recover from it, are far more likely to be able to give the kind of leadership that recognises the strengths and needs of their group.

Even with the most sensitive leadership styles, the leader faces potential isolation. Whereas once one was in a circle of equals, now one's thoughts and utterances carry an extra weight – they are no longer like everyone else's; they are special. But there can be a penalty for being special: on the one hand, one may be envied; on the other, one may be thought not to have the same (or, indeed any) problems, as though one has moved into a different kind of human category.

In truth, while leader and led do have different agendas at different moments, they have more in common than is often remembered. The difficulties arise when individuals unknowingly abdicate aspects of their own personal authority – vesting it in their leader – or when the leader takes the authority of the position as a vehicle for personal power, forgetting that it is the aim of the project that is at stake.

Leadership works best when it both responds to an articulated desire and takes that desire further forward – when it shows why we have to change, or take up this difficult route, or jettison this particular way. The Hague leadership is ridiculed because it seems to be leadership in a vacuum. While Hague has a notion that his party should listen more and care more, they seem interested in power and authority, but it is hard to know exactly what for. They are bruised, for sure – we get that message – but what do they want to do if they get back in

Government? Does anyone actually know, or is it leadership without a purpose? People trying to think about new ways to organise themselves often reject the forms of leadership that are instantly available. They try to find ways to respect individual authority without that degenerating into a tyranny of non-leadership in which no decision can be made unless there is absolute agreement. The frustrations implicit in such a style can easily lead one to conclude that structured leadership is more effective, but there is no guarantee that it is. Plenty of organisations flounder because their leadership saps the energy of those outside the inner circle; they can't get in, they can't contribute, their input is not valued.

It will be very interesting to see whether Scotland can produce a political structure that builds on the very initiative that made self-government attractive, and in so doing create a new form to reflect the individual and collective needs of the people.

Dependency Culture

Set aside, for the moment, the purely economic arguments for limiting aid to Montserrat and its citizens, or for reducing payments to single mothers. Listen, if you will, to the words behind the headlines entreating us to see these people as subtly but intrinsically different from ourselves.

It's not that there isn't a natural sympathy for them. It's not that all our hearts don't bleed when we hear how hard their struggles are. It is so much part of our humanity to be able to respond to people in difficulty that a counter-argument or ideology has to be surreptitiously promoted before we can get our heads around the idea that people who are in need or difficulty or suffering are in some way undeserving.

It's hard to see quite how this happens, how initial reactions of empathy and concern can be blown off course to the extent that just hearing the words 'dependency' and 'single mother' leads us at once to anticipate a whole set of unsavoury associations, mainly to do with unworthiness, greed, poncing, malingering, taking advantage. And if those ideas fail to take hold and individuals persist in their empathic stance towards those in need, those individuals are taunted for being over-idealistic or naïve. Or, in a more sophisticated twist, those who want to push for substantial economic aid are held to be paternalistic and backward.

What we're all meant to understand now is that since self-help engenders self-respect, then its opposite must inevitably engender despondency. And since few can quarrel with the evidence of the self-respect argument, the conversation is deemed closed. Those who want to raise wider issues of the relationship between countries in difficulty, individuals or groups of people in need, don't really get a serious look in. But aid is not, in fact, necessarily the opposite of self-help. Self-help *is* what people do every day. They don't have to be persuaded to help themselves; it's in the nature of survival. Few fail to try, although they may be more or less competent at doing so, and some may disagree with the routes of their self-help. It's effective help that provides dignity.

Judith Williamson has written persuasively about how language gets sanitised and subverted to conceal the viciousness of a status quo in which there is a huge imbalance in resources. But the question remains: what are the psychological states that make unpalatable ideas digestible, and what are the psychological mechanisms which enable us to interrupt our natural responses? How is it that we can be moved from a position of empathy to one of suspicion, indifference or rejection?

Whether it is a volcanic eruption, a tale of bullying, encountering the poverty of many lone-parent families or the loss of a child – when disaster strikes or enters our awareness, our empathy is twinned with fear, worry and helplessness. We immediately project ourself into the disastrous situation, where our sensibilities are emotionally aroused. It's not so much that we are altruistic but that our concern and caring arises out of a (fleeting) imagining of ourselves in such circumstances. Yet at the same moment that we feel compassion, we may also experience fear and helplessness.

It is in the difficulty of simultaneously holding on to our feelings of concern and those of helplessness that we become vulnerable to arguments which deposit poisonous ideas about the painful circumstances of others. Words that mean something benevolent in one context – such as in our own family and friendship groupings – come to take on an entirely different shading when applied elsewhere. We label them as dependent, encoding in that word a set of attitudes which are contemptible, as though dependency were something countries and people should disdain and avoid. This is then bolstered by a moral argument that seeks to elevate independence, without recognising that independence itself rests on mutuality and engagement.

None of us is or can be independent of one another. Our interconnections, our relationships, our embeddedness with each other is a central aspect of human experience. When we turn away from people in need by labelling them 'dependent', we are using an ideologically tainted word to cover up our own helplessness and our fear that we can't do much to help. Of course, there are many situations in which we can't do that much. Montserrat may be one. But what's so impossible about owning up to that? What's wrong with a position that expresses compassion, offers what it can, and acknowledges the limitations of aid? Isn't that preferable to the acutely hypocritical moral position in which we see ourselves as bountiful but those people over there as somehow not quite deserving?

There may be a similar dynamic behind the important initiatives to get young people and lone mothers into meaningful paid work. It may be that the present Government feels less able than it might wish to transform the enormous social and economic problems it has inherited. It could be particularly galling and frustrating for those in public service, whose motivation and *raison d'être* is to control and shape the public arena, to encounter any degree of helplessness. Action is the mode of politics. But in the face of frustration and the very real difficulties of transforming our society, could it be that a handy but unpleasant ideological hold-over from the past two decades – where those in difficulty were consistently besmirched – remains unchallenged because it is a sop to the (unrecognised) helplessness we all feel?

I don't believe that the present administration wants to insult those in need. But I do wonder whether politicians faced with so much desire to transform and so much frustration wouldn't be better off taking another tack: one that accepted the limits within which politicians can change things and respected those scorned as dependent. We'd do well to reverse the sense that things are being done when they aren't or can't be, or where the solutions are difficult, complex, unclear or even not immediately obvious (as in Montserrat). Far better to acknowledge limitations – which is a way of negotiating with being overwhelmed – than to hurt further those whose difficulties have touched and moved us.

Politicians desperately want to include those people who are currently excluded for various reasons because it's awful both for them and for society. A campaign that supported and highlighted their desires rather than the fact of their burden would be more dignified and respectful, as well as psychologically and politically honest. It would also be a lot more effective. People currently not in paid work – be they lone mothers, young people or the middle-aged – have ideas, hopes and wishes that are often thwarted not just by the economic conditions but by the ideological baggage they are asked to carry. More honesty about what resources can and can't be put forward could join up with the desires and initiatives of those currently excluded, which would release the energies that are available, rather than squash them. It would stop the pretence that all is perfectable, and at the same time it would remove the taint of blame in the air that does nothing but deceive us and widens divides in our society.

Secure Attachments

As disciplines develop, new paradigms emerge to shape the contours of understanding. The paradigm that surrounded Freud's work and psychoanalysis has been under pressure for the past 30 years. Freud's far-reaching discoveries showed that it was possible to dissolve symptoms such as paralysed legs, desensitisation of the skin or painful contractures of the arms and hands by deconstructing, via the talking cure, the meaning of the symptom.

Freud's innovations were so rich that for many working with psychoanalysis it was possible to build on what he had created without explicitly rejecting his metapsychology and instinct theory. But under the surface, there has been a shift towards seeing attachment processes – the actual interaction between infant and carer(s) – as central to the mental development of the individual. This may sound laughably obvious to the non-psychoanalytically oriented reader. Of course, the actual relationship is central. That's why we endeavour to parent well, why we believe in good care for children as opposed to bad care. And, of course, this belief is very strong within psychoanalysis.

But attachment ideas, until recently, have jostled with ideas which postulate that human beings enter into their family of origin already endowed with ruthless emotional, sexual and aggressive energies (libido and the death instinct); energies that are tortuous, unstable, deeply disruptive, surprising, invigorating and so on. From this perspective, human development is, in one sense, a process of management of unruly instinctual desires.

In contrast with an instinctual view, or growing up alongside of it, is a more relationally-inclined understanding of human development which holds that the human infant is oriented towards relationships. This view regards the baby's entry into the world and its subsequent development as being highly dependent on the relationship(s) it is offered. The relationship is experienced and internalised by the infant. The growing child then goes on to shape its expectation of other relationships based on the complex of feeling states aroused in its original relationships.

To put it simply, a child who has experienced an anxious carer is likely to be anxious in making other relationships and will bring a sense of uncertainty to those new relationships. In addition, it may spend much (unconscious) energy attempting to look after its carer, either in the hope that the carer can do a better of job of looking after it and/or because it feels guilty that it has depleted its carer by being simply too much.

The attachment or relational paradigm has slowly emerged within psychoanalysis over several decades. It is associated with the names of Suttie, Fairbairn, Bowlby and Winnicott from the clinical end in the UK and more recently in the research work of Mary Main, Mary Ainsworth, Daniel Stern, Peter Fonagy and Colwyn Trevarthen. The empirical work has confirmed what many psychoanalytic psychotherapists have observed and worked with in therapy: the central role of the earliest carer's psychological and social circumstances as a determining feature in the developing individual's sense of self, confidence and capacities. An anxious carer creates the conditions for anxious attachment; an emotionally disorganised carer the conditions for chaotic attachment, while an emotionally secure, responsive carer the conditions for secure attachment.

As well as focusing on the central role of the earliest carer's psychological and social circumstances as a determining feature in the developing individual's sense of self, confidence and capacities, Attachment theory has entered the public space to proclaim itself as a basis for social policy. But once there it has rather mischievously and, I fear, mendaciously, been misappropriated. In post Second World War United States there was the appropriation of a misogynist version of Freud in which the soft cops of the psychological establishments attempted to re-channel female vitality into the 'Apple Pie Mom' to avert unemployment among men returning from the war ('Give us back our wives and sweethearts'). Today in the UK we can observe attempts to link attachment theory with calls for the reinstitution of the Heterosexual Nuclear Family.

Attachment theory is not about reviving the two-parent family which has buckled under difficulties of all kinds over the past few decades. Most of the so-called family refusniks, or critics of the family, were products of that brief historical moment in the West when the family consisted of two parents whose roles and responsibility were highly differentiated and unequal. They rejected that family. It didn't work. For many of its members it was highly problematic. It failed its women (remember Valium), its men (remember alcohol) and was unable to encourage its children to reproduce it.

Far from being a stable reassuring form that people want to duplicate, the family threw up critiques and modifications of all kinds. Feminism, now assailed for its central role in the family's demise, had many different stances towards it. But a position that many psychologically minded feminists called for, based on an understanding of the human need for commitment and continuity, was not the abolition of the family but its reinvention in which when men made the decision to reproduce, their involvement with children, doing consistent co-parenting, would be central.

It was well understood two decades ago, when the 'traditional' family was already showing strains, that adults and children prosper when they have secure attachments. When one can trust relationships to stay in place, to support and underpin one in a reciprocal manner, one is free to explore, to be curious, to create. Secure attachments are what most people seek even if their backgrounds have disposed them to enacting versions of early anxious or chaotic relationships. Attachment theory makes sense because it addresses difficulties people and institutions have in getting on with the business of being.

Attachment theory tells us a lot about what a preventative

national mental health policy could look like, how it could be translated into the family of whatever kind, into educational, economic, political and social policy. What it absolutely doesn't tell us is that it can be a ballast for recovering the canonical nostalgic family of yesteryear.

Attachment theory is about the quality of relationships. But it is being used now as a rhetorical device to mop up tough and difficult discussions about ways in which people's emotional well-being can be achieved.

We need serious conversations about all kinds of families, about how we raise our children, the implications of insecure employment patterns, the impact of policy changes every few years on our institutions and personal psyches, and so on. Secure attachment can be offered to the next generation when the adults feel secure themselves. Let us investigate the conditions which can make that most possible rather than slide over truly difficult economic, social and personal issues in a call to the happy family that rarely was.

Intimacy in Public

You feel you know the person, yet you don't. You know lots of things about them. You know their faces and how they move, you recognise their voice. If you chance upon them outside the context in which you have come to 'know' them, you look at them again and again. You're not staring so much as trying to get a direct experience of this familiar person that you know and don't know. Their presence, whether actor, politician, musician or sports hero, is disconcerting and exciting at the same time. They are no ordinary stranger.

Into this gap, this distance between not knowing the person but feeling they are part of our landscape, we pour a whole set of ideas, projections, fantasies and hopes as though the densities of our desires can close the peculiar span between knowing and not knowing. By visiting on this visible stranger our own notions of them, and by attributing things to them and analysing their behaviour with reference to our own, we are endeavouring to personalise them, to make an individual – even intimate – relationship with them. At the same moment that the person is set apart from their peers by fame, so we try to make them 'one of us' again, with our wash of fantasies.

Why is fame such a feature of life today? What are its functions? What does it do for us and how do those who seek it, or who are the recipients of fame, manage it?

It's possible to see fame as an interface: expressing the tension between diversity and uniformity that seems present as the world becomes simultaneously larger and more accessible while increasingly impersonal. The ever-swelling proliferation of the images of a very few individuals, groups or brand names appears to allow individual and cultural differences to coexist. What the images of the Spice Girls, Reebok, the Pope, Nelson Mandela, movie stars and musicians conjure up is a sense of belonging and identification: the wish to bond with others and the seeing of something of oneself in the image. In a global world, they function as messengers reasserting the clear identities akin to those of a village.

Sometimes, the product or the individual encodes a political agenda or a set of moral principles. Sometimes the person carries for us our deepest aspirations and hopes for humanity. Sometimes the image carries sensual or stylistic aspirations; sometimes rebellion, sometimes survival. The figures that hold together our global village are cemented by the collective feelings we bestow on and attribute to them. Whatever the message or the multiple messages with which we endow our cultural icons, honouring and elevating them is a way of placing ourselves in the world.

As our world has become increasingly complex and popu-
lous, and as the history of the physical world is shown to be ever
longer, it's hard for each individual not to feel some confusion
about his or her individual significance. As a chance occurrence
in evolution, humans are far less successful than bacteria. We are
but one tiny life in a world of trillions of lives. We may feel
rooted and recognised in our local communities, with friends
and family or at work, and gain a sense of security from such
attachments; but even so, we may not know how to work out
the meaning and purpose of our own lives and how and where
they intersect with that of a world population. This inconse-
quentiality is further emphasised in a culture that celebrates
and invites individuality. Dwarfed and confused about our significance or insignificance, we bestow emblematic importance
on selected strangers. They become stand-ins for the individual
importance we are unable to feel or have recognised. As they
become larger than life, we – through our identification with
them – challenge our own insignificance. We enhance them,
which in turn articulates how we feel each life should be
enhanced.

Beyond our need to recognise our own significance by
attributing to strangers (whom we then remake in our own,
idealised image) the stature which is eclipsed in our individual
lives by the sheer enormity and impersonality of global life,
there is a need to understand ourselves.

Through fame we make someone, some people or some
thing represent us. We then project on to that icon the conflicts,
struggles and dilemmas of everyday life. The way we then pre-
sume they handle their predicaments acts as a reference point
for us. We debate the merits of what they have purported to do,

what they ought to do, what we would do in their position. We criticise and praise. We act as though we have first-hand knowledge of their particular circumstances – a state that eludes even the closest of close friends. Although such mental meanderings can seem idle or foolish – debating the rights and wrongs of what a television character does as though they were real – we engage in them because they are a way of knowing ourselves better. We discover through the other what we think, what we might do, what we are perhaps feeling.

The iconic stranger performs the function of letting us project on them our fears, our trials and our quandaries. Where we are confused and sometimes overwhelmed, we find or visit on a 'famed' individual a dilemma that mirrors or reflects in some ways our own. We have the distance then to work out the intricacies of what to do: what is morally and emotionally the way to proceed.

These projections which we make on to the famous are often unconscious. We endow them with special gifts and capacities that elude us, or which we may wish to emulate. We may then admire their ability to manage what we find so difficult. In elevating their (presumed) capacities, we are saying something about our own strivings and the human desire to celebrate that which expresses the very best of us. The obverse is equally true. We can begrudge this unknown known their apparent ability to handle what we can't. We assume their ability – although we can't and don't know – effortlessly to enjoy what they have. We can then envy them like characters in a fairytale. When they stumble, or rather when we see they have difficulties, we may feel compassion for them, but we can also feel relief because their mortality and 'ordinariness' have been returned to us.

For the 'famed', it's not so simple. Mass-scale recognition is nearly always out of proportion to accomplishment, and there is no way an individual can absorb this kind of attention. Fame is difficult to handle; it has little to do with the individual. The exaggeration of praise, the adoration, is often felt to be undeserved. Even those who craved fame and then received it can find it hard to absorb: it can feel undeserving, unreal. A hunger for fame and recognition isn't hard to understand; it is one possible response to feeling unseen and disregarded.

At a psychological level fame exemplifies an attempt to reverse the sense of invisibility so endemic today. In the act of awarding it, we imagine we are rewarding and praising the best of who we are, while restoring the hope of being individually seen and accepted.

Moving On?

A t Cambridge in the 1930s, his passion for social justice
and workers' rights made him a natural member of the
Communist Party. At 30, he saw this as naïve and turned to the
Right. With the same enthusiasm as when he'd fought for the
Spanish Republic and against fascism, he now attacked any-
thing liberal, progressive or socially inclusive.

In her youth, she protested against women being sexually
objectified – why should women corset themselves into clothes
that are too small, deny their appetites and spend hours and
pounds on beauty preparations? As a 60-year-old, she applauds
facelifts, tummy tucks and hormone replacement therapy.

In his twenties, he was a hippy with a conscience working in
a health-food shop, buying from Third World co-operatives,
preaching that small is beautiful. Now, he's an investment
banker who believes that his leveraged buy-outs create the

wealth in society. 'You'll see,' he says to his environmentally concerned son. 'Your values will change when you see how things *really* work.'

But is that true? What is happening when we change in ways that make a mockery of what we were before? What psychological processes are going on when experience causes us to reject and ridicule our early commitments? It's easy enough to see that enthusiasm for social change can become eroded. The wonderful confidence of youth – grabbing a world it feels sure it can change – may be worn down by the overwhelming power of the world as it is. We might prefer it if people and governments were more receptive to change, but unless we accept just how powerful and entrenched social forces are, we run the risk that not only any attempt at change, but also the spirit to transform itself, may be crushed.

If we recognise a social reality which we abhor, and if we have the self-awareness to acknowledge the way in which it works on us as individuals, how it undermines our confidence in our ideals, we have a way in to making common cause with others who feel similarly. We see what they are responding to because, in part, we feel the same way. Then, instead of using a tremendous amount of energy in rejecting utterly what it is we condemn in society and in steeling ourselves against conforming, we can use that energy to confront some of the difficulties involved in making effective change. We need neither disavow our aspirations, nor deny the difficulties.

Of course, the greater our experience of life, the more elaborate life's complexities are. Then we can find ourselves acting in ways that are at odds with our stated desires. Growing up, as opposed to ageing, means managing the clashes inside us and finding ways to accommodate our shifting roles – daughter, worker, mother, say – and hence our changing perceptions. Growing up, in its best sense, means expanding our views in ways that take account of complexity. It's not that we see how things 'really' work in a simple way, but that we see how things 'really' work in their complexity, without needing to repudiate viewpoints we have long held because they conflict with later experiences.

Youth holds out the promise of remaking the world. Our ideas about what's wrong can feel so clear and our actions so right and just. It is difficult to acknowledge that the social structure is sufficiently resilient and adaptable to incorporate some aspects of what we were fighting for, while at the same time dismissing the core beliefs from which they spring. It is how we cope with this difficulty, with the unfolding complexity of life, that determines whether our ideals can evolve or whether they are rejected and reversed.

Those who see how persuasively social reality moulds our desires – and willingly accept the process as a way of engaging with what is happening around us – are less likely to be buffeted by the exigencies of the moment. Instead, they create a pause for reflection. In tranquillity they find the capacity to embrace complexity rather than being overwhelmed by contradictory impulses and feelings.

The ex-political activist who now disparages the ideals he once held, the woman whose feminism collapses in on itself so she now embraces what she once railed against, the hippy turned ideological banker – they show us how difficult it can be to hold on to ideals in the face of the pressure to accept what is, and the difficulty of acknowledging one's own impotence.

Of course, change *per se* is not necessarily problematic. Life constantly presents us with the opportunities to refine, refresh and develop. Such change can be embraced in a satisfying way if we don't belittle our previous ways of understanding. However, it is the dismissive denial of a former position – such as with our three examples – that tips us off to undigested change, when complexity and disappointment can't quite be managed. If someone gives an account of personal change that is respectful or tender towards their earlier self, then we all understand and respect that change. But if they disparage who they were or in patronising tones tell us how naïve they used to be, then we are witnessing a defensiveness which is there to bolster uncertainty, squash down questions and ward off that which doesn't fit.

Omnipotence and helplessness are two sides of the same coin. A belief in one's correctness and invincibility is often a way to counter feelings of helplessness. Helplessness can appear devastating and constricting – an emotional place too close to depression, emptiness, or despair. People find all sorts of ways to fend off or bypass helplessness; they swing away from it with anger, with blame, with repudiation. From the outside of the feeling, helplessness seems so crushing, so defeating, that one may never wish to experience it. It smells of victimhood or weakness. But from the inside, helplessness is a stepping stone into the more tender emotional states of vulnerability and humility. These feelings don't so much diminish us as give us a kind of solidity and integrity which underpin us.

The problem is that if helplessness can't be accepted for what it is, if human beings are unable to recognise how small and insignificant they are, then they are likely to use what power they have with a shrill officiousness. Rage will be the glue that holds them together. The exercise of power from this basis can be very cruel because it is so defensive. It can be effective, but still a power that masks a vulnerability.

Derision, denigration or disavowal towards youthful positions are much more worrying than a change of mind. They are not a sign of maturity at all, but an indicator of instability and insecurity. Paradoxically, maturity means knowing that you can't quite know everything as confidently as you believed in your youth.

The Great British Disease

Envy in Britain is a curious phenomenon. Accompanied by a desire to see the other fail, to wait for and enjoy their comeuppance, envy is almost a national sport. Newspaper columnists thrive on it, comedy draws on it, a stratified society provokes it.

So deeply entwined in the British psyche, it is hard for many to recognise how automatic the response of envy is – and how corrosive. It takes a trip abroad to see its uniquely British shape. Envy in the United States, for example, is a more robust creature; there, envy links in with a galvanisation of one's own desire, it's a spur, even an inspiration.

In some cultures envy isn't part of the vocabulary. It is recognised as a motivating feature of emotional or economic life. This is in contrast to the amount of space envy takes up in the British psyche, within the political ideology of today, and within psychoanalytic theory. Envy in Britain is muddled in with protest about social and economic inequalities, with an inability to activate personal desire, with the rancid effects of the class system.

The legacy of living in the most stratified Western society is that the categories of envy have been used in perverse and peculiar ways. It has never been all right to envy those who have lots more. Those are the people we are to respect. But it has always been all right to knock your neighbour who, by chance or opportunity, has been more favourably graced. Envy within the layers is encouraged. Envy across the layers is disdained.

People's outrage and protest about the management deals made in the recently privatised utilities break this rule. Hence the slogan 'the politics of envy'. In this phrase, the Tory Ministers are trying to shift righteousness. They are trying to convert their guilt about the enormous remuneration being paid to chief executives while the remaining workforce is diminishing, on to the protesters by calling them 'spoilers'. They imply that it is the protesters who don't want British industry to succeed, that it is the protesters we can fault for the failure of British industry.

This tug on British emotions can work because as a nation we are indeed very confused about achievement and success. When Britain was 'Great', national pride served to provide social cohesion where in fact tremendous conflict existed. The collapse of national pride foregrounds an especially British phenomenon: the difficulty we have with celebrating accomplishment. In Britain, success of various kinds is tinged with a worry, as though there is something unseemly about it. Certainly one shouldn't openly enjoy it. Guilt, self-deprecation and apology are the appropriate handmaidens to accomplishment.

But where do this reticence, chagrin and embarrassment come from? Is envy the problem, or is accomplishment? Or is it the relationship between the two?

When acting on personal desires was the preserve of the privileged, an emotional receptivity to self-suppression was a reasonable form of psychic protection for the rest, a defence against what couldn't be had or expressed. It wasn't simply that the many were suppressed (which, of course, they were), it was that they made their lives and expressed their passions within particular spaces. The maddening injustice of the disparity in opportunity was then psychologically expressed through anger and through envy at those who were like oneself but who could break out of the confines, who tested the boundaries, who dared to break the rules internalised by most.

While people may have struggled in various groupings to change their situations, in their individual lives some comfort was gathered from being able to manage within the limits, to control personal ambition, desires and so forth. This was certainly true for many many women who, while hating the limitations on their lives, found ways to survive and flourish. But if a woman stepped outside she was branded, was experienced as threatening, as breaking the code in which women voluntarily kept themselves to a conception of femininity as constraining as bound feet.

But surely in today's so-called classless society, it shouldn't be like that now? Surely we shouldn't have our best paid and most enjoyed writers pilloried for their success, or for their wish to bring about more social equality? We shouldn't have the upcoming generation of feminists ticked off by their elders, sneered at by their peers? In another country, such people would be celebrated, not only for their personal accomplishment but for its symbolic significance; for what it says about what is possible for any of us. Envy in other countries retains its ties to admiration. The person who has achieved success is supported and their admirers draw strength from them. It inspires them. But here a meanness abounds. We wait for those who have succeeded to fail. We even hope they will.

Meanness was once concealed behind a moral agenda that criticised greed and envy. Part of that morality has an ethic that can speak to us today. It is against waste, flagrance, ostentation; for community, sustainability, regeneration. But much of that morality was used to bind up people's own conflicted desires – desires felt to be so dangerous that they couldn't be explored, thought about, day-dreamed over, understood, possibly acted on. Instead they had to be banished and girdled. The desires were suppressed and denied. Meanness came in their place, creating a lack of generosity towards self. This pinched quality then permeated one's relationships to others. The difficulty with feeling all right about enjoying one's imagination turned into a crusade against desire, against having, against wanting and into a disdain for those (of one's class, sex, race or age) who did and had.

Envy, and the experiencing of others' accomplishments as a diminution of self, is part of the legacy of denial that flows from situations in which resources divided iniquitously are supported by an ideology that fails to challenge this divide. Envy is an understandable response.

People who protest against inequitable pay settlements for the few are showing that they are offended and angry. Politicians naming that as envy are mischievous. But the personal envy that is stirred when others (rather like oneself) do well, is worth thinking about so that the meanness it engenders could be transformed into the energy to allow the imaginative space to be filled with one's own desires rather than voided by the sourness of envy.

SECTION III

Family

What Kids Want

It's a tricky business, this getting money and values sorted. Especially when we are talking parents and children. Time was when lots of money was bad, very little money was difficult (but morally acceptable) and values – what you believed in, what you stood for, whose side you were on – were what counted. There were numerous good sides to choose from: literature, nature, politics, general worthiness, honesty, diligence, a hard day's work, family, poetry, civic duty, the union, darning not wasting, generosity. The social classes had their own codes for identifying what was of value and what was beyond the pale.

Money was OK for those who had it, although best not to flaunt it unless you were in showbiz. But money was not OK for those who didn't have any. You weren't meant to aspire to it. Remember the contempt in which the *nouveau riche* (the code for those who earned rather than inherited wealth) were held, what detestable kind of money they had? Remember, too, those patronising reflections on the way poor people could so ill-advisedly spend theirs? Or worse still, so ill-conceivedly aspire to wanting it.

In those days of pre-consumerist Britain, how you related to money, to wanting it or depreciating it, was a reflection of character, of your moral fibre. Although capitalism ruled, there was an alternative set of values through which people felt they expressed themselves. It was pursuits rather than consumption that mattered. Poverty wasn't idealised, but neither was it seen as the fault of the poor. It was something to be remedied by social engineering.

But as Britain has moved from a producing to a consuming society and the social contract is rewritten, so the relationship between money and values is shifting. While market forces have always dominated much of our lives, the British class system curiously kept a lofty distance from money so that values and money appeared if not unrelated, then, for many, antagonistic. Naïve perhaps, but it certainly was a lot easier for parents to try to raise children with a coherent set of values.

Values are now punctuated by market forces unhindered by the veil of propriety. At every turn, from the packet of crisps offering £10,000 to the Lottery to the salaries of sports heroes and supermodels, the desirability of big money is instilled. Woe betide the parent who questions the wisdom of the emphasis on money: 'You're sad, Mum.' And just as 'sad' now means pathetic, so money has come to mean value.

It is hard for a parent today, especially when the economic climate is so desperately unstable. You either struggle to get enough money together to look after your family or, if you have enough, you try to suggest that this commodity that rules so much of our lives, our identity and our relationships, is not such a many-splendoured thing. But you're up against a reality which says it is about the most important thing there is.

It used to be that money permitted choices – choices that often disparaged the love of money. But kids today construct their realities around the things only money can buy: football strips, toys, clothing and equipment that proclaims the name of the manufacturer. At younger and younger ages, certainly younger than any of their parents, the search for identity and self-expression takes form within consumer culture: the right Nike trainers, the right Barbies, train sets, rollerblades. Children learn corporate recognition before they know their three-times table. In the United States it is estimated that children of 5 can recognise 1,000 brands (not many flowers or trees though).

What hope for parents, old-fashioned enough to care about different values? How and what can they do to intercept the thrust of childhood corporatising? What can they say when they are alarmed about their children's admiration of the big salaries, big cars out there? And what direction too for parents who themselves have been part of the radical change of attitude; those who grew up in families where either there wasn't much money and it wasn't especially lusted after, or if there was some, it was very much in the background.

Many such people have now come to enjoy shopping. If they have surplus income they like grown-ups' toys and are susceptible in one part of themselves to the considerable talents and creative energies of producers and marketers who aim to contradict the old messages that values and identity can't be bought.

If parents are drawn to self-expression in this way, how can they convey messages that separate values and money, and how can they impart a sense of value for money, for pleasure in selected treats rather than constant consuming?

Many parents remember the pleasure of anticipating a treat, of waiting for their next birthday for skates or a bike or a football. Such purchases now can cost proportionally less than many years ago and are in a sense more easily affordable. Are we promoting false values when we tell children they can't have a new set each season?

The inevitable separation between generations is accelerating and making itself felt in a new sphere – consuming. While parents nostalgically indulge in memories of a continuity of values that existed between them and their parents and grandparents, there is a divide between their children's perception of what is important in their world and what parents deem important. In this difference lies the issue of both parental responsibility and parental separation.

Of course parents have to convey a set of values to their children. They do this in the way they behave and through what they say. To abdicate would be to fail to be a parent. But parents also need to be able to enter a child's very different experience of what constitutes the norm, or survival, or what is 'cool'. Here delicacy is required. Berating a child for their desire, calling them greedy, selfish, a spendthrift or just plain gullible for being turned on by what the ads promote, makes the parent appear withholding. A parent's alternative point of view is then unlikely to get heard as anything but prohibition. But if instead of condemnation or a simple no, parents engage with the child's perception, they can then both support and distinguish themselves from the child's desire. If they can convey that they understand the child's wanting: 'I can see that you really want that T-shirt, and I wish I were able to give it to you,' then they can go on to say no. To not respond to it if it conflicts with the parental value system, or to finesse the issue by saying that you can't afford it (when you can) rather than saying you don't want to buy it, deprives both parents and children of a chance to experience each other's differences.

We may disapprove of the extent to which the market-place has come to dominate certain aspects of children's social relations; but if we wish to present a different view, we have more chance of being effective when we don't make children feel guilty or bad for their wishes, and when we can tolerate the differences that are bound to occur between us and our children. Giving kids more than a parent feels comfortable with is no solution. In its denial of difference, it stores up trouble for the future. Generations thrive together not because their wants are seamless, but because they understand each other.

Smacking

The debate on smacking, unhelpfully posed as one in which an adult has the right to determine how a child should be disciplined, has avoided discussing what motivates an adult to smack. Seen at a distance, one might suppose that we regard children as a separate species who require different things in order to thrive, or as free spirits who require breaking in. In extremes, children are cast as monstrous or angelic icons of innocence.

This polarised vision of our young as Rousseauian naïfs or as 'bad seeds' confuses the discussion. While it accurately expresses an adult's chagrin at their lack of understanding of a child's desires and behaviours, it sends the discussion in a direction that makes children people to be done to, rather than human beings we want to get to know. We push them around instead of finding ways to share and exchange our perception of life.

Our idealised view of children is an expression of the goodness and sweetness which we as adults rarely see articulated in adult society. In the idealised state, it feels as though adults and children are 'us and us'. We take pleasure in their goodness and sweetness. Their charm and creativity reflects on us, engendering feelings of well-being and positive identification. When this idealised view is disturbed, an alternate set of psychological operations comes into play. Then we are at risk of relating to them as little monsters, as 'us and them'. We engage in a power struggle in which we are seriously at odds with each other, at times even hating them, and we are susceptible to shouting at or hitting them.

Josh, aged two, and his mother Sara returned from their holiday on a Sunday morning to discover that their telephone had been cut off and the building work in their flat had severed their water supply. There was unexpected chaos everywhere and a lethal smell of chemicals from treatment to the windows. On the journey home, Josh had chatted on excitedly about seeing his room and playing with his toys. When Sara saw the state of the flat her heart sank, but after ranting into space, she galvanised herself and went to the phone box to try to normalise things. After several unsuccessful attempts, she gave up, and was walking with Josh back home. He started to whinge and Sara gave him a smack on his bottom. This smack startled him and horrified her; she burst into tears and apologised: 'It is not your fault, darling. Mummy's very cross and upset with the builders and BT.' Sara recovered herself and went on with the job in hand, but was perplexed by her behaviour. She had never hit Josh before: she disapproved of it. What was it that had made her lash out?

Sara did not smack out of a desire to discipline her child. She wasn't teaching him right and wrong – as the justification for smacking is habitually posed. She smacked out of her frustration, her disappointment, her anger at the situation that faced her and Josh on their return home. As she thought about it, she recognised that she had dealt with the builder's nightmare as capably as she could, but it had taken all she had not to collapse, to remind herself that she was the one in charge of the situation. She realised that she felt as whiney inside as Josh; she was disgruntled and put out. She had wanted to return to a habitable home and she had wanted Josh to have a smooth re-entry after a long absence. She was tired from travelling and tired of encountering new situations. Her pleasure at having coped with the difficult scenarios that travelling with a toddler can provoke was punctured by her sense that she had nothing left inside to give. She couldn't manage any more. It was this feeling that she couldn't manage, together with Josh's disappointment, that sent her 'over the edge'.

The smack was a mechanism to release her pain. As long as Josh was quiet, the visibility of their shared distress was out of view. When he complained, her unconscious identification with his distress forced her to encounter what she couldn't bear to feel. The slap was to silence both his pain and hers.

Sara's story underlines a common emotional scenario for smacking. An everyday example occurs when the agendas of a parent and a child clash. The child is being a nuisance in the supermarket. The parent has used all her or his creativity to manage the situation. The sweets or toys at the check-out counter are a magnet for the child's desires which have not been met in the aisles. The parent is holding herself tight, keeping a lid on her wishes and just trying to get through the tasks. When her child acts spontaneously and its randomised wanting attaches itself to an insistence on sweets, the parent loses a grip and shouts. Or smacks.

But what kind of discipline is this? We aren't teaching children right from wrong. We are teaching them how to stop revealing or expressing their desires. Of course the child wants his or her own goodies in the supermarket. From their perspective, we've been loading up the trolley with our goodies, we've had the pleasure of choosing the boxes. Now it's their turn. Why shouldn't they want the things that appeal to them? In place of smacking or scolding, we need to recognise the inevitability of their desires being stirred up. 'It would be lovely to be able to have all those things in your basket, Gaby, can you choose one that would be just right for you?' If this can be accepted by an adult, then they will feel heard and understood. The child is more able to accept that even though it wants ten goodies, it must select one for now.

It is a child's enthusiasm for his or her wants that can set off a difficult psychological trail in the parent. If the parent is unable to allow that want, if they have learnt to bottle up their desires by feeling that they are wrong – rather than desires that can sometimes be met and sometimes not – then a child's expression of desire is agonising. They have to be silenced, for they activate what the grown-up has stifled in him or herself. And it is because they have had to suppress their own desires that they find the constant giving-in difficult and the management of a child's wants draining. The adult still requires confirmation that its own needs are all right: but being unable to find that, they expend much psychological energy binding up their own feelings, and are psychologically exhausted and alarmed when the child expresses his or hers.

When we smack or feel impelled to, we might ask what our child is expressing that we find so hard to handle. Has it anything to do with right or wrong, or is it our attempt to get the child to bury needs and desires we've learnt – albeit in a fragile way – to control in ourselves? If we can intercept our wish to strike a child, we can view the impulse as a reminder that we need to attend to our own desires and create an emotional ambience in which differing emotional needs can be acknowledged and respected.

Smacking II

'To smack or not to smack' is never out of public discussion for very long. With plenty of evidence that smacking is at best ineffective and at worst harmful, it is worth asking once again why we smack and what we are expecting the smacking to achieve.

Smacking has been portrayed as the studied decision of a grown-up who, reflecting on all the alternatives available, has decided that a smack will be the best method for putting a stop to a child's offending behaviour. But, as any parent or carer – and any child who has been smacked – will know, smacking is rarely premeditated or thought through.

Indeed smacking, like many other sanctions, occurs inconsistently and spontaneously. Sometimes a particular behaviour will bring forth a smack, and other times it won't. As a method of informing a child about 'what is right and wrong' it is pretty useless. The sanction so depends on the carer's state of mind that a child will have difficulty decoding exactly what the smack is about.

The child who is consistently smacked for a particular reason does come to know that its unwished-for behaviour will have consequences. But it is not the smacking which provides the message to the child, it is the consistency of the parental action that carries it, and this is a key to finding alternatives to smacking.

Smacking is most often the automatic and unpremeditated response of a parent or carer who has been worried or frustrated. The smack is not intentional, but an expression of feelings which cannot be released or expressed in another way.

Often the parent or carer who smacks is someone who has been smacked themselves in their childhood. The model they were given for handling frustration or worry or annoyance was one in which the smack signifies an attempt to silence or banish the difficulty. Through physical expulsion of the difficult feeling on to another, the feeling was dispersed.

Now in adult life, faced with a child who causes worry, frustration or annoyance, the parent finds her or himself smacking. In enacting a version of their parents' behaviour, they overcome the powerless feelings they had as a smacked child, while simultaneously disassociating themselves from the troublesome behaviour of their own child.

Children quite typically get smacked when their parents are fearful that they have been in some danger: for example, when they wander off or hide for hours. Is the message to the child that such a smack is about their self-protection? Surely not. The child is confused. If the parent was so worried about me, why did I get a smack? Is a smack to be equated with worry?

Smacking, then, is never about the child *per se*. It is about the adult's feelings at the time. For those who only exceptionally smack, the subsequent guilt which can result lets the parent know that it was their feelings which were out of control. So, before we kid ourselves that smacking is a thought-through response to a situation we wish to change, let's recognise how much a smack is motivated by the parents' state of mind at the moment, their unconscious identification with their child, their wish to separate themselves from their child's behaviour, their assumption of a parental image taken from their parents but not necessarily questioned, and so on. Smacking is far from a rational decision; nor is it a corrective to unwished-for behaviour. It marks a failure to enforce the needed boundaries between parents and children.

When adults smack children, they are attempting to demarcate certain behaviours and to let children know that there are boundaries that they should not traverse.

The boundaries that parents and children seek are important. A lack of boundaries creates a state of confusion which makes it hard for anyone to know what their limits and responsibilities are. When families are too enmeshed, smacking creates the physical expression of separation. But this separation can be achieved more helpfully by parents and carers being clear about their responsibilities and the expectations they have of their children.

Alternatives to smacking, of course, require thought and diligence. They require attention to parenting, a skill we undervalue and one for which we imagine ourselves to be magically prepared by dint of having children. But for many parenting is the hardest job in the world, and part of the difficulty comes in being unprepared and having only the model of parenting we experienced ourselves to work from.

If that's been reasonably satisfactory we can employ it with ease, but if our own childhood made us question our parents' methods then we have few alternative models to draw from. As fashions in child-rearing lurch from the so-called permissive to the authoritarian, parents can feel completely at sea.

Over the last few decades, research by psychologists, teachers, child therapists and analysts shows that if we give children very clear and consistent messages of what we expect from them the children will more willingly fit their behaviours to expectations. Adults in charge can support this by showing the child their appreciation of the children's attempts to follow the framework that is offered.

The alternative to consistency creates frustration. Let's take the parent who wants the child to feel responsible for clearing up its room and it wants the child to do it without prompting and nagging but it just proves so difficult to convey this that the parent gives up. In the parent's head, it is endlessly forgiving towards the child for not clearing up until one moment it snaps and either shouts or smacks a demand that the child clear up. The parent has not given a clear expectation. In fact sometimes the parent tidies the child's room itself to relieve the tension it feels about the mess. The parent hasn't really thought through what it wants from the child or how to achieve that relatively harmoniously. In effect the parent is coasting emotionally hoping that it won't mind too much if the child does or doesn't clear up. But at some point, of course, the parent does mind and the sanction of smacking or shouting follows. Consistent clear expectations could have relieved both sides of the heartache ensued by the inevitable smack.

The alternative to consistency creates frustration, out of which adults resort to smacking. This is a signal indicating an area of parent-child interaction that is or feels out of control. By earmarking areas of frustration and setting out to find solutions that rely on the transmission of clear expectations, backed up by parental recognition and appropriate praise, much frustration and the ensuing wildcat smack can be set aside.

'You're so
embarrassing . . .'

You're walking down the street on a fine spring day. The flowers are smiling and the conversation flows. You stop to coo over a kitten in the arms of a stranger, make small talk, and then move on. Everything is fine, or so you think.

Your 13-year-old turns to you, firing a bullet of hate and contempt at your heart, throwing you off course. Now you know what's meant by 'if looks could kill'. But it doesn't stop at looks. The emotional force of the utterance which follows bowls you over.

'How could you do that? That's disgusting.'

You're bemused, confused and quite a bit miffed. 'Hey, what did I do? What's going on here?'

You try to steady yourself, but the assault continues. She grimaces. 'You are so embarrassing, Mum. Why did you have to do that? Why do you have to be such an idiot?' Wondering whether, or how, to censure your child, you keep quiet, reflecting on adolescence. And especially that awfulness of your parents getting it all wrong and humiliating you. But before the reverie can continue so that you can find some way to understand rather than kill your child, she starts up again. A litany of your misdeeds follows to rebuke you. Of course, some are hurts that can't be aired any other way, and so you know you'll have to wait it out.

Adolescence is an awkward time, when the wish to define oneself as distinct from one's family jostles with a continuing need of them. Almost anything a parents gets slightly wrong can feel excruciating. As the young person sculpts her or himself, they become acutely aware of what they don't want to be like. When something jarring asserts itself in the parent's identity, it is as though the young person's self-image becomes contaminated. She now feels the parent as a massive boulder that needs to be pushed off, and separated from. So raw and unformed is the new adolescent's personal identity that it can feel crushed, or at least injured, by parental actions. Cooing over a kitten shames them; they wouldn't be seen dead doing that. In chastising the parent, the child is distinguishing itself from such silly actions. Their very being would never countenance such things.

The adolescent involved in the struggle to make her or himself into their own person can't imagine that their parents can understand anything. Of course, they were never teenagers, were they? They were children – the pictures are there to prove it – but young people coping with changing bodies, explosive emotions, deep uncertainties, and passionately interested in sex, music or drugs? Never that. Parents are parents. Parents metamorphosed from childhood to adulthood without the intervening struggles. And teenagers need to see them that way – as stable, adult, permanent people to bounce away from. The boulder image works both ways. The adolescent needs to get out from under it, but also needs the boulder to stay in place as something that is fixed and durable.

One minute, the child wants the parents' understanding. The next, it excludes them from the emotional Wurlitzer that is their daily experience. There is separation and heartbreak on both sides. The parent revisiting the mood, smell and poignancy of their own teenage years feels compassion for what their child is going through. But the wisdom of growth is unwelcome to the child who has to make its struggle in its own terms. It wants parental understanding, but it can't bear it and finds itself shaking it off or discouraging it. This is not a time when many adolescents can openly or consistently admit to needing a parent. And although they can take from the parent, usually in the cracks between eruptions, the parent and teenager together have to weather a perplexing and agonising time.

Adolescents are trying to separate psychologically from their families, but if they haven't received enough of what they require, their process towards separation will be very ambivalent. The young person still yearns for caring, containment, understanding. They are confused about who they are. If the family is unable to manage the intensity of feelings that bursts forth as the teenager tries to connect outside the family while remaining attached within it, it is a nightmare for all involved.

The emotional states of adolescence seem all-encompassing. They are dramatic, intense, cataclysmic. Everything is lived in capital letters. Such emotional states have something in common with what parents have called the 'terrible twos', when the toddler is trying out an earlier phase of separation. But the intensity of a two-year-old is more manageable than that of an awkward, sexually-interested 15-year-old who may well tower over their parent.

In adolescence, we try to redo and remake what went wrong before. If we felt emotionally deprived, we search desperately for emotional connection. If we don't get it, we seek it through drugs, sex, intense friendships or joining groups with a strong identity. Or we resort to restructuring the self. The epidemic of eating problems among adolescent young women is one attempted solution that simultaneously mimics and rejects the way in which femininity has been cast in our culture. Behind the problem, the fragile personality identity is encased. It can't articulate the enormous pain the transition from childhood to adulthood is for females. These young women speak with their bodies about the contradictory pressures they are trapped within.

For boys, the path to adulthood is no less complex. Indeed, with the crisis in masculinity manifest all around them today, the sense of who to be often has to be created in a vacuum. The pull to create a personal identity via a group that both tests and attempts to confirm that burgeoning masculinity is very strong. Gangs and their class equivalents are very attractive, because they are a way for boys and young men to rework their dependencies without appearing 'weak'. It is as though the group speaks to the dilemma of attachment and intimacy for boys, where often the absence of involved men in child-rearing has made it hard for a boy to feel comfortable with his attachments unless they are linked to strength.

But adolescence is also an exuberant time, when a generation makes its claims on the culture and tries to influence it in its own image. It is necessarily a time of contestation, of flamboyant rejection of what is. Adolescents' actions demand that we look at the world anew. In the adolescents' rejection of our morality, our aesthetics, our music, our politics, our literature, they force us to interrogate our own tired responses. If we can just hold steady and let our children differentiate while staying connected, we may yet become refreshed ourselves without having to live through that special *angst* that is adolescence.

Almost One of the Family

For many young children with working parents, this is the time of year when au pairs, mother's helpers and nannies leave. Many families are used to the annual goodbye coinciding with the end of the school year. The adjustment is straightforward. An *en famille* summer holiday is followed by the welcome in September of a new person into the household, a new class teacher and growing responsibilities for the children. But leavings and changes are never without an impact, and it is well to think about how all these changes can affect everyone so that the transitions can be as smooth as possible.

For a child who has spent a considerable amount of time with his or her au pair – being picked up from and/or taken to school, played with daily, put to bed by and so on – a rapport and closeness has built up which can be painful to lose. Although children who have gone through the annual changeover of au pairs may be accustomed to saying goodbye every July, there is a wrench. If we can allow space for the child to feel the emotions that may ensue with the imminent departure of an au pair, then the child will neither have to harden him or herself against the hurt this causes, deny it or collapse into a depressive loss. If the parent can talk freely about the impending departure of the au pair and the kinds of feelings that might be experienced, then the child knows that whatever she or he might be feeling is all right. Where children are told at the last moment that someone is leaving, where they are teased for being sensitive – 'There's no need to make a fuss about Anya leaving, you felt just the same last year and then you really took to Birgit!' – they absorb the injunction not only about expressing their feelings but for having the feelings in the first place.

If censorship prevails over natural responses to loss and change, it is hard for the child to assimilate such feelings and they may become afraid of separation. In turn, this will affect their capacity to make bonds with others, as the fear of loss will loom as an unmanageable psychological event. If, on the other hand, conversations can be embarked upon by a parent in which the possible sadness the child or children might feel when 'Anya leaves' can occur, then the child's recognition of its feelings can find acceptance outside itself, and there will be a home for its feelings inside itself too.

Of course, there will not only be feelings of sadness or loss. Sometimes, an arrangement has been difficult for the child, so that relief is an additional (or even the main) feeling. When children are uneasy with a situation and their unease is not addressed, they can take on the idea that in some way they are the cause of their own distress. Having a chance to acknowledge relief to the parent helps minimise any unconscious guilt on the child's part that they are the cause of the unsatisfactory arrangement.

When sadness, loss and even relief can be acknowledged, the child can make an internal mental adjustment to accepting the situation. It isn't fighting its feelings or having to get angry, disruptive or withdrawn to find a circuitous outlet for them. Instead, they can be processed and contained.

The situation also needs attention from the au pair's point of view. Au pairs are young women who might have come to a foreign family looking for a stepping-stone to separation from their own family. They want independence and perhaps a nonintrusive type of family experience which can be hard to get at home. They become part of the household but not enmeshed in the family. Entrusted with the substantial responsibility of caring for children while parents are working, they have to do this in a situation where they may have had a tortuous journey to win over children who – mourning the loss of the previous young person looking after them – have felt less than receptive towards them.

This is not uncommon. However skilfully the family has managed the departure of the old au pair and the welcome of the new one, the new au pair – in a strange environment where complex social and emotional issues have to be negotiated – can experience the children's lack of receptivity to her, and their elevation of the wonders of their previous au pair, undermining. But for the most part, and in successful arrangements, over the course of the year the au pair develops good and close relationships with the children and with their parents. They now need to disengage from them, and they may be unsure about what future contact the family will encourage and accept.

Even an au pair who is excited to be returning home or going on to college will experience a loss which needs to be recognised and respected. The parents can give guidance about what kind of contact would be welcome, both for the au pair's sake and also to maintain a sense of continuity in the children's lives.

Au pairs often have an extremely hard job. They arrive with limited English, they are away from home for an extended period for the first time and they have to find ways to fit in with their families. The au pair has to assess the rules and nuances that abound in the family, how to judge when she can go to the fridge, sit in the living-room, be part of the family, vanish from the family and so on. That achievement and sensitivity is rarely praised. But when it is, it can be very supportive.

And finally, what of the host family? In the best possible arrangements, the parent(s) will have made a good relationship with the au pair and so there may be feelings of sadness, or wistful regret that they are moving on. Where a particularly close bond has occurred, a family may be unwilling to let an au pair go, and out of this desire a range of distortions can enter the situation.

Some hosts may have felt the arrival of the au pair was like gaining another child (albeit a grown-up one). This may have engendered dynamics that seem inexplicable on the surface. The au pair may have projected issues from her own family on to the host family; by the same token, the host family may have projected on to her their own feelings about their late adolescence; their approval or disapproval of her.

Of course, an au pair who has been experienced as difficult for the parents while wonderful with the kids (it does happen) poses problems of great psychological tact. The parents still need to make space for the missing feelings that the children or the au pair might feel. This requirement to address the loss is perhaps the most important task that the host family has to take on for everyone. In making space for it in conversation, in inserting awareness of it into the ongoing life of the family during the last weeks leading up to the au pair's departure, loss and separation can be recognised by all. A good goodbye can happen, and the relationships can be held inside all our memories with an accuracy about their importance rather than the confusions which occur when denial surrounds departure.

Empty Nest

The time immediately following the departure of children who have left home to go to college or university can prove to be one of great adjustment all round, involving considerable challenge to the parents left behind.

For years, a woman's loss when the children left home was patronisingly derided as 'the empty nest syndrome'. When we first started The Women's Therapy Centre 23 years ago, we met many women who had been offered a prescription of Valium and advised to redecorate their home as a way to make the adjustment.

But encoded in this prescription were two hidden messages. One was that only women (and especially women whose primary preoccupation was their children) suffered loss, and that fathers were relatively immune to this distress.

It doesn't take a genderquake to recognise the sexual politics implicit in this diagnostic pattern. And it doesn't take more than one or two conversations with parents and siblings to recognise the enormous significance of a young family member leaving home.

As long as we label the phenomenon 'the empty nest syndrome', we can collect all the distress that exists in the family and apportion it to Mum. But if we really want to live through this period fruitfully, we have to take account of the complexity of everyone's feelings surrounding this event.

It takes more than a few weeks to adjust to the changing situation. This is a period in which aspects of everyone's future – the child who has left, the parent(s) and the remaining sibling(s) – are being mapped, but flux remains the order of the day.

There may be feelings of instability. Younger siblings, eager for a different recognition in the family, scramble to replace or supplant their elder brother or sister. They may crave a new kind of attention or feel impelled to fill the vacuum created by the departure.

Almost everyone can feel both bereft and needy in the family, and the temptation is to unconsciously designate one family member as the bearer of this distress. The problem with this solution is that neither the family as a whole, nor the individual members have a chance to surrender to the emotional changes they are going through. A kind of ossification occurs which makes the family dynamics brittle. The chances for both shared and separate responses to change are curtailed.

Particularly underestimated is a father's loss at a child's departure. James found himself extremely interested in his young secretary a week after his son Adam had left for university. A large gap threatened his equilibrium because his son had provided much friendship and closeness as well as a link with youth. He enjoyed being both adviser and companion to Adam. They had spent weekend time together, and the connection with this youngest son was the most vibrant relationship in the household for him.

On his son's departure, he ridiculed his wife's tears and utterances about her loss. His attention was drawn to his secretary, whom he began taking to lunch and for drinks after work. Her interest in him and her admiration of him buoyed him up. With her, he could be the mentor – an important aspect of his relationship with his son.

But he could also present and discover in himself a playful side which had lain dormant for many years. The re-emergence of these qualities and his eagerness to experience it kept him away from home and the void that he was unable to face there. His loss was side-stepped.

While driving to visit his son at university, his wife Olivia forced a discussion of Adam's absence and insisted that she couldn't be the only one who was finding their new circumstances difficult. She disclosed that she had felt depressed and lonely, and although her work was as interesting as ever, had found her attention wandering and her lunch hours caught up with unnecessary trips to the shops to find that little something which would make everything feel so much better. Her vulnerability touched James; he found himself unaccountably crying and they pulled off the road to have their first real conversation together in years.

Where his feelings had been temporarily diverted towards his secretary, they now came into view directly and appropriately with his wife who had borne and raised this son that they were now both missing. This poignant coming together is less common than it might be. For many couples the *raison d'être* of their relationship has passed or the capacity for renewal became exhausted. The individuals have developed in ways which outgrew the couple, and the commitment to the children – once fulfilled – releases the individuals to find new identities and living arrangements.

But for many couples like James and Olivia, the void can be used to rediscover one another and to hold and nurture each other through this phase of life.

For a lone parent, the loss can be devastating. Like any parent, part of them may have longed to be released from the daily tasks of parenting, and at the same time they may have felt immensely pleased for their children who are leaving home and taking up their own lives.

However, the loss may be more acute than anticipated. There is not just the loss of the actual company and relationship, but the removal of a structure in which their life has been governed, for the demands of lone parenting mean that little flexibility is possible and the necessity to always have in mind the needs – be they domestic or emotional – of the child were a defining feature of the adult's life.

The release from this may unsteady the adult until they can begin to put in place other meaningful markers for daily life. When a child leaves home, all the attention is on his or her departure. But once that child has left, the focus needs to turn to the multiple processes occurring within and between the remaining family members so that their emotional needs and responsibilities are creative rather than simply reactive.

Blood Sisters, Different Parents

It is common to assume that, as they grow up in the same household over a similar time-frame, siblings have the same parents. Certainly, at times such as Christmas when families get together, brothers and sisters may emphasise and treasure shared experiences. They may value their parents' fine qualities, their sense of humour, their foibles, their generosity, and so on. Equally, in families where the Christmas gathering can be fraught, alliances may be created between children against parents whom they find difficult. Shared perceptions, negative and positive, are part of family life.

Children grow up together and become who they are by absorbing – and making their own – the idiosyncratic patterns of their particular family. But, within the same family, children's experiences can be sufficiently divergent for us to say in many cases the parenting they received was very different.

The dissimilarities of children's experiences often get eclipsed by the notion of the family. But, in fact, each child in each family does have a different set of parents. The grouping within a family is constantly changing, and parenting is a dynamic relationship. Being a parent embodies one's individual history and personal desires. Each parent has a set of intentions as well as projections – conscious or unconscious – towards each child.

On the face of it, Rose was the beautiful, intense and moody daughter, and Julia, her younger sister by three years, the charming, funny, clever one. These designations on the part of parents are not unfamiliar. Attributes are perceived in children, who without much difficulty recognise these qualities and seek further confirmation. Billed as charming, funny and clever, Julia was quite able to meet these expectations. Similarly, Rose's intensity and moodiness reflected and reiterated a psychological space she could occupy. The parental division of characteristics found a version in each sister's self-perception.

Much has been made of the way in which parents assign different qualities to each child. Indeed, we could start the story there and explore the implications of such divisions, but I want to go beyond this well-trodden territory and attempt to look at the dimension of experience that lies behind parents dividing up their children's attributes. I want to bring into focus the way in which each child (or, in our case, Julia and Rose) experiences the distinct and unique ways in which their parents treated them. From Rose's point of view, she had parents who hovered, were quite anxious and interfering. They seemed to swoop in on her and bring a tension into much of their relationship. Her transition from nursery to school, from primary school to secondary school, their attitudes towards her clothes, friends and interests were imbued with worry. Although Rose couldn't quite put it into words, an atmosphere of 'Will she, will we get it right?' permeated the air around her and her parents. Rose's own intensity and moodiness reflected her response to her parents' worries and to the ambience they had created. She magnified their concerns, dramatised them and made them her own. Where they had fussed about whether she would ever wean herself or tie her shoelaces, her relation to self involved distrust and unpredictability. She felt she couldn't quite rely on herself, she didn't know where her moods and passionately strong feelings came from.

For Rose, then, her parents were nervous and intrusive. They created an environment in which anxiety burgeoned. Rose became the child who confirmed that anxiety, and integral to her sense of self was a cautious, almost distrustful, nervousness.

Julia, on the other hand, the second-born, had a rather different set of parents. Although still worried about whether Rose would get her degree, find a mate, secure interesting work, have babies and so on, so that every transition continued to be clouded with anxiety, where it came to Julia they had internalised a certain confidence about themselves as parents and accepted that children do find their own way through things. While the parents were unable to apply what they had experienced with Rose to the next stage of Rose's development, Julia was the beneficiary of her parents' growth. From the beginning of her life, Julia's parents had brought a surety and confidence born of the previous experience of parenting. Although they had worried that their second child would inevitably receive less attention than Rose, they found that they were relaxed and spontaneous with Julia in a way that they hadn't felt able to be with Rose.

The self-assurance Julia's parents brought to their relationship with her, their knowledge that what they had to give was sufficient, their trust that she could survive, made the atmosphere around Julia completely different from that which had surrounded and continued to surround Rose. Julia's development did not arouse anxiety. She was given more space; she wasn't watched over nervously, so that she was able to find a rhythm which evolved from being securely attached rather than constantly impinged upon. Julia's parents reinforced this view of her as capable, and she grew into the competent, charming and rather more curious young woman than Rose was able to be. Rose was dogged by a sense of self that oozed caution and worry. Julia's parents longed to be able to apply what they had learnt with Julia to their relationship with Rose.

Last Christmas, the daughters inevitably disagreed about their parents' qualities and there was considerable tension. Rose's distress was voiced and, as she gave an account of her experiences, her parents were able to amplify this with their own assessment of the differing ways in which they had treated and continued to treat each child. Although they were unable to undo what had occurred, they were sad about these discrepancies, and over the year the recognition of these rather rigid dynamics had helped all of them to reflect before responding. They wanted to be able to give Rose what they felt she had missed: a quiet confidence in herself. They awaited next Christmas in a more open state of mind, hopeful that they could all use their insight to transform themselves.

Suffer the Little Children

How are we to understand the recent news of injuries – seen on closed-circuit video in a hospital – inflicted by parents on 39 infants, some as young as two months? Are the parents who endanger their children particularly vicious and sadistic? Are they deriving pleasure from their actions?

What about 'ordinary' parents, who hug a baby and feel great love one minute, only to experience massive frustration and hate the next? Is there a continuity between the feelings that can visit any parent or close carer of a child and those of the parents observed hurting their babies? Is there a relationship between our difficulty in absorbing the horror of children being tortured and the conviction of Louise Woodward for second-degree murder?

Many people, when confronted with what happened to Matthew Eappen or with video evidence of child abuse, don't want it to be true. To confront these tragedies means to face a whole set of beliefs and ideas we have about how adults, especially parents, are naturally protective towards children.

The discovery of paedophile rings in Belgium was devastating not just because it is repulsive, shocking and terrifying but because, for so many of us, the idea that one could actually engage in such acts is completely incomprehensible. Child torture not only arouses feelings of disgust and revulsion, it seems to be of a very different order from the negative feelings any parent can have towards their babies and children.

Because we live in a century of childhood and – since the Sixties – a time when children's needs have been seen as significant, it is hard to remember how recent the notion of childhood and childhood innocence is. Only a hundred years ago, infanticide was not uncommon. Only recently has corporal punishment – the caning of children as somehow educative – been banned. Not so long ago our Prime Minister felt quite comfortable saying that he has smacked his children. The idea that children deserve respect, that they deserve to be free of physical and mental abuse, that what is in their minds and in their hearts is interesting, that their opinions matter, is one we are just beginning to take on fully.

So many of our views of children today retain a vestige of the time when they were thought of either as little adults who needed no special care (and thus could be sent up chimneys, down mines, or expected to conjugate Latin verbs at four) or as adults' objects – there to be experimented on, to be moulded in this way or that, or to serve adults as needed. If we can bear this history in mind, then the indigestible aspects of child abuse – and the psychological issues that cause us grief when we try to come to terms with what has been exposed in these 39 video cases and the need to find a 19-year-old guilty of child murder – sit in a more comprehensible setting. If childhood is a recent historical phenomenon, so too are our attempts to make sense of child abuse. Such a framework doesn't make the horrors any more palatable, because they can't be, but sets a context in which we can try to come to terms with what has been exposed in these videos.

Ninety-five per cent of the harm done to these infants is attributable to their mothers' actions, as picked up by the video cameras. Yet the mothers showed great concern for the children's injuries when they spoke with others. How can we put these two things together? Is this simply a case of remorse masquerading behind the women's 'pretend' worry that they will be exposed? I think not. Indeed, remorse may not even come into the picture.

If we look at the compassion, concern and attention these women received through their children being ill, we may begin to understand something of what motivated their attacks. Some researchers suggest that these deeply troubled women are using their children as a means of obtaining attention which they feel they have no other way of receiving. It's not that these mothers consciously harm their children because they know they will get cared for themselves, but more that they have learnt that the only attention available to them is through illness. There is evidence to show that some of the mothers were probably victims of this form of brutality in their own childhood, and that kindness towards them came from the concern of others. They were used by *their* mothers to express unconscious conflicts. As mothers themselves, they did what was done to them: inflicted on their children a version of their experiences of being parented.

At a deeper level, we need a way to understand the inner world of those who parent in this violent, murderous way. We are getting more accustomed now to thinking about what girls and women who hurt themselves – either through cutting their abdomens, arms and legs or by extreme bingeing and purging – might be doing. Although in the first instance we may see these acts as self-destructive, we can also understand the way in which they are a vehicle for the very unhappy person to try to deal with her pain and conflicts. By hurting their bodies they make their pain concrete, while still keeping it private and inside them.

To comprehend women who harm not themselves but their babies, we might get somewhere by linking two things. First, there is the fact that hurting oneself can be soothing to those who self-harm, that the cuts which a woman makes on her body may offer relief because she has caused her own pain rather than being the arbitrary object of it. Second, there is the fact that many women have difficulty in seeing their babies and infants as separate from – rather than an extension of – themselves: their babies are both of them and not of them. The baby's pain may provoke their own pain, and in using the babies to express this, they lose psychological sight of the fact that their babies are people with feelings themselves. In the depths of a deep and frightening disturbance, harming their babies may be a way of harming themselves.

Every parent can be subject to murderous thoughts towards their children. This is an aspect of parenting; in that sense, there is a link between all parents, those who abuse and those who feel. The tragedy for the parents who harm is that they may not feel this normal sort of rage. If they could feel it, then they could accept it in themselves as part of the range of feelings that intimacy evokes in us. But their rage is so overwhelming and unconscious that it is split off from their conscious selves, so that it bypasses thinking processes and can only be given expression in action. It isn't processed, it can't be thought about, it can only be acted on.

It would be nice and clean to draw a clear line between the rage that any parent and carer can feel towards a child, what Louise Woodward is alleged to have done and the acts of the 39 parents seen torturing their children. Indeed, when we convict, that's what we do; we find a perpetrator and stop thinking. But what these two events force on us is the need to think more deeply about what's going on when we are aroused in such disturbing ways – and what it is that parents require in order to receive attention themselves, as well as to receive help and support in parenting.

Divorce: When Kids Can Get More

It was a relief to see some research come into the divorce debate, in place of the same fallacious platitudes being endlessly trotted out about how irrevocably damaging divorce is for children. No one opts for divorce without anguish, but for some it is the only realistic – even the better – option. What the latest survey of studies by Rowntree confirms is that it is the *quality* of the relationships between ex-spouses, and parents and children, that matters. It's the continuity of a caring and present relationship that is crucial.

However, that is not so easy. Parental separation poses real challenges; divorce is difficult enough even for the adult who has precipitated it and even when no children are involved. Friendships are broken, economic circumstances often worsen, the individuals have to create separate lives and households where once their social and psychological identities were entwined.

Rebuilding a self after a fractured relationship is a long and difficult process. Fear, depression and panic, along with feelings of displacement and loneliness, can make a person coming out of a committed relationship feel temporarily crazed. The pain and rupture can be so debilitating that the individual is disoriented. Managing oneself, building up new supports and feeling at home with a changed identity takes time. There may be periods of social withdrawal and periods of hypersocialising as one's confidence waxes and wanes. There is little that can be counted on except the emotional roller-coaster that separation (desired or unwanted) precipitates.

If this is confusing for the adults, imagine what a tailspin the separation of parents creates in a child. Even though children of parents who fight may have consciously hoped for a divorce and even suggested it to their parents, when the parents actually separate the disruption is profound. Even when the children stay in their home, what has been the known, the norm, disappears either gently or violently along with the sense of what parents are as a unit. Despite the increasing normality of parental separation, there is explaining to do to oneself and one's friends. There is the confusing pull between wanting to know why and wanting to know nothing, between feeling emotionally abandoned one moment and emotionally invaded the next, between the known and the secure and the unknown and the confusing. The world as the child has experienced it has evaporated.

Such a picture might sound as though divorce is the last thing anyone should contemplate. In the short term, it is bleak, disruptive and destabilising. But the fact is that, for some people, divorce in relation to children – while initially anticipated as the only but worst option – can in fact become the

better option. For some parents, the relationships they are able
to make with their children post-divorce are infinitely preferable
to what went on when the couple were together.

What never gets discussed in the divorce debate is the way in
which unhappy couples visit on their children not just the
model of an awful relationship (thus tilting their views of the
possibilities that can exist between adults), but the effect of
that awful relationship on the individuals concerned and how
that then impacts on the parenting.

A man unhappy in his relationship, with options to stay
away from home through long hours at work and socialising,
perhaps with an affair thrown in, is not only an absent father –
the absent present father – but he is also likely when at home to
be somewhat uneasy, possibly guilty or even defensive about his
absences in an aggressive kind of way. He may tell his children,
'Daddy wishes he could be with you more', which is a certain
truth, but he may also convey to them and his partner a reluctance about being home. His absence in itself makes it hard for
him to spend time with his children, to know their needs and
adapt to their rhythm; they have a life into which he has to find
his way. Relying on his partner to make the relationship with
the children, he piggy-backs on to her relationship with them or
one that is shaped and mediated by her.

A woman unhappy in her relationship rarely abandons her
children on a daily basis in the same way that a father can.
Even if absent, she will likely have made the arrangements that
structure the children's day and be in touch with their activities.
But a certain resentment may seep out of her about the dissatisfactions which exist in her relationship, and it may be hard for
her to be with the offspring of her deteriorating partnership

without conveying the disappointments and often the contempt she feels for their father. The urge to offload and therefore inadvertently skew the children's experience of adult relationships and of their father may be well-nigh irresistible.

To be sure, it's no picnic when parents split up. The parents don't suddenly behave better, become super-mindful of the children and do everything in their best interests. And certainly there are disaster scenarios a-plenty in which 30 per cent of fathers (and very occasionally mothers) disappear, or where children move from their locale with no accustomed supports except a depressed and economically displaced parent. But this isn't the only outcome. In all its difficulties, divorce is also an opportunity.

What makes the opportunity hard to take up, however, even given reasonable economic factors, is if the separated parents continue to relate to one another as if they were still each other's disappointing partner, and if they exacerbate the complicated loyalties aroused in children by a parental separation.

The first golden rule for continual decent contact is that each parent should act towards the other parent – when they are with the child or children, or making arrangements about them – as though they were people with differences who respect one another. This involves not carrying the feelings of hurt, anger, betrayal, sadness and confusion (which usually accompany a split) into their present relationship with one another. Despite the fact that the ex-partners are bound to retain all their irritating ways towards each other as they try to manage the children whom they have created together, it's important for each adult to discuss those irritations with people other than their children or their ex-partner. Being bonded by disappointment, hate or hurt is not only damaging for the adults but very perplexing for the children. It makes the world incredibly unsafe, for it belies the point of the break-up: if they are still so antagonistic, then what is the real reason why they split? The child's answer to that question is, as you can imagine, me. But if the parents can co-operate and be civil, the child or children can have confidence that change isn't only a disaster, relationships don't *only* fail and, most importantly, they themselves were not the cause.

The second golden rule is consistency. Not necessarily consistency in seeing the children every Wednesday or Saturday – although that helps – but in being available to the child in his or her life and insisting on maintaining the relationship even during those times when the child doesn't want to see the parent. It is the parent's ability to make and hold on to the relationship that provides the child with security and enables it to talk about what may be confusing or awful in terms of the separation.

There is plenty of evidence now that fathers (particularly) who are able to hold on to their kids in the face of the very real difficulties that exist may be having a far richer experience of what it means to be a father than they did when they lived with their children. Instead of relying on a relationship via the mother, taking the relationship for granted, fitting in and being helpful, they now share time and create their relationship with the child directly. They get to know their children and themselves in ways which extend them rather than slot them into the limited framework in which they may have related before.

When this happens, the mothers are released. Their longing for a partnering parent may not be happening in the relationship, but then neither is their resentment. The children are no longer burdened with the mother's view of the father who is never good enough. Children of separated parents may have it different, but many of them are getting clearer and more direct relationships with their mothers and fathers than would have been possible had the family stayed as a conventional unit.

The Universal
Scapegoat

For nearly all of us, our mothers are our first relationship. It is in her arms, with her words, her food, her emotional ambience that we are introduced to the world. At first, of course, she *is* our world. We apprehend its shape, the way things are and how things feel through her presence. She is embedded in our very sense of self. We become individual human beings by imbibing who she is inside us. So deep is her influence that we may not recognise its extent, or if we do we may wish to limit it. And even when we resolve to do things differently, we may discover ourselves acting as she did, reproducing her attitudes with our own children.

Mothers have been both glorified and vilified. In the early days of feminism much attention was addressed to their pervasive influence. This was partly an attempt to focus on and reveal the actual (rather than the idealised or maligned) position of women, the majority of whom become mothers. It was also partly an attempt to understand the mothers whom we felt disappointed by, burdened by, angry at, responsible for and often guilty about. We discovered that in the mother's social role – in her job as socialiser of children, unpaid household worker and emotional treatment plant for the family – there was a huge price to be paid: literally, in her economic devaluation, and also legally, socially and psychologically in her position as a subject.

Mothers and mothering were analysed from a variety of perspectives – not least of which was a consideration of the influence of the mother–daughter relationship on a daughter's emotional life. The endless cycle of mothers mothering daughters who must go on to become mothers themselves was taken as a point of entry in understanding some of the psychological aspects of the reproduction of a psychology for women that could accommodate women's social role.

Today mothers are under attack like never before. If they are lone parents receiving benefit they become a scapegoat for social and economic problems not of their own making. Their lack of a man who can provide is evidence of their cunning and immorality. The message today is that society needs fathers and families – and indeed it does – but what is forgotten is that the family has changed, and what constitutes the family, and what we mean by mothering and fathering, is being reformulated in the lives we lead. While the upper echelons continue to abdicate parenting themselves by sending their nanny-reared children to boarding schools when they are merely eight years old, true to the mendacity of current politics their representatives in Parliament advocate hands-on parenting for the rest of us.

This kind of focus on mothers is very different from that of modern feminists who have been trying to understand the social position of mothers in order to comprehend, structurally challenge and avoid reproducing the difficulties that exist for women. Feminists are not interested in attacking mothers, but in exploring what the consequences are for all of us in a society that devalues women, underestimates and mythologises the work that goes into mothering, and takes for granted the fact that most parenting will be done by women on their own.

But it is not only in politics that mothers are under attack. Inadvertently, many psychotherapists can all too easily fall into the trap of blaming mother – abstracting her from her position as an individual and social subject, and viewing her solely as the failed object of the patient. Of course it is inevitable that, in a discipline that takes as its field of study the 'how we are who we are', our first and most pivotal relationship will take centre-stage at some point. It is inevitable, too, that some of the distress, longings and conflicts from that key relationship will be replayed in the therapist–client relationship, whether the therapist is male or female. Each person brings their history to their present. We make and shape present relationships with reference to past experiences, and anticipate acceptance or rejection based on an emotional knowledge of what has gone before.

In exploring inner conflicts and conflicts with others through the therapy relationship, mother can become the object of the patient, reduced to two or three opposing generalities – usually good and bad, giving and withholding – as opposed to the multi-dimensional subject she is. With both satisfying and problematic experiences being felt from babyhood on, the individual sees her or his mother as a bifurcated enabler or disabler of their desires.

Since fathers or other adults have, in the generation who are now adults, played generally more minor roles in the day-to-day upbringing of their children, their meaning as an alternative relationship in the psyche is correspondingly decreased. To be sure, fathers matter and are important springboards for different kinds of relating, but they may become less liable to the fierce splitting that characterises much of our internalisation of our mothers. This internalisation is what has given mothers a bad name.

What theorists of psychological development can fail to take into account is the extent to which mothering is both a social and a psychological process. As we listen to the stories in the consulting room, we unavoidably form pictures of mothers who could not easily recognise their children's needs. But it is all too simple for therapists (and ministers) to then blame mother rather than set her perceived inadequacies in context.

Instead, professional case conferences and much psychotherapeutic writing still unwittingly blame mothers. In family therapy, we are still blaming mothers for being over-intrusive while failing to insist that men engage more in parenting. The mother in therapy is often described as cold, controlling, withholding, manipulative, smothering, over-identified, ambitious and interfering. And, while all these appellations may have a good deal of accuracy, the emotional presence they are attempting to describe suffers from being in shorthand; a curious phenomenon in a discipline that takes great care in elaboration.

Therapy runs the risk of describing what it sees without

contextualising it. Politicians may be happy to use this cheap and nasty device, but those of us in the business of understanding need to do more than describe what is. We need to understand the process of mothering in its contemporary setting. If we do that, we can talk more accurately and usefully about the trouble between mothers and daughters, mothers and sons, and mothers and fathers.

It is only when we can be compassionate towards our mothers' efforts to meet the often unrealistic demands placed on women in our culture – while at the same time fully recognising the failures of our parents – that we can truly understand ourselves.

Who Remembers?

S he looked down and realised he'd forgotten his physics book. Yesterday it was his trainers. 'Shit,' she cursed. 'Testosterone.' Her 17-year-old son was forgetful and spacey. She alternated between blaming his dad, whose forgetfulness drove her crazy, and maternal self-recrimination: 'Maybe it was all the remembering I did for him that stops him remembering for himself.'

Forgetting encompasses many different states of mind. Forgetfulness and what is often posed as its opposite, remembering, are complex psychological events. Why do we impute moral value to the rememberer and impugn the forgetful? What things are not only all right to forget, but also dangerous and antisocial to remember? What things must never be forgotten? And how does remembering and forgetting fit in with a culture gripped between a disposable present and a recycling of history as nostalgia, a remembering of what never existed?

Freud's great project was to understand the processes of repression. To analyse the whys of what did or didn't get remembered and where events went to if they were emotionally unfinished. The inability to forget, the problem of being plagued by unwelcome memories, with being stunned by disparate fragments of experience: smells, moods, ambience, the lack of coherence, as well as the difficulties with recalling, forms the bread and butter of a therapy. As the Freudian story goes, we are destined to repeat what we cannot remember. Similarly we are tormented with inconvenient and intrusive remembering when we have emotional indigestion.

Some experiences can be felt in ways that are untroublesome, while others become split off, repressed, dissociated or insistently carried in mind, taking up much of the available psychological space. In so far as we can manage a variety of emotional experiences, we can allow ourselves to be affected by the new. The novel has an impact; it changes and refreshes us. In so far as we can only manage a limited range of experiences, the new becomes transformed into a version of the old, the known. New experiences cannot then infuse us. Rather, we re-label them as old experiences in new clothes. Repetition becomes a form of psychic solace. These seemingly automatic responses – our psychological reflexes, so to speak – can be mediated by purposeful attention. Observing what we do, frame by frame, allows for different kinds of openings: what Freud so famously called working through. By minutely examining what we find ourselves doing, we have the possibility of changing.

So what happens in the psychological economy of house-holds or relationships, where one person appears to remember for the others? What was encoded in the mother's mutterings about her son and husband's forgetfulness? And how is it that women so often stereotyped as scatty are, just as stereotypically, vested with remembering? Is there some truth in that mother's lament that it is her remembering which has stopped her son remembering for himself? Is remembering a quality which can be handed around, divided up?

The spacey son and the forgetful dad could only be describable in those terms when Mum was around. Mum would manage and make sure that everyone's sandwiches, books, messages and money requirements etc. were organised. These were ordered according to her standards and, although she resented all the doing, she derived some satisfaction from her management skills and from having these domains to control. She was always extending herself, thinking into the next requirement, what these men might need in x circumstance – even when x circumstance was well outside her experience. Remembering or thinking in advance for them was a way to insert herself into their lives which were separate from her. She might not be directly involved in their joint or separate activities, but the planning for what they needed (which was what remembering meant for her) was a way to be a part of what they were doing. She might not go fishing but she acquainted herself with all of its paraphernalia and requirements. They were bound to feel her presence with them, and she felt her connection to them as she did the preparations for them.

For their part, the men, while not especially aware of what she was doing (and, some might say, taking it for granted), only became aware of her efforts when she wasn't around to do it for them. In her absence, they would go into a tailspin of looking and retrieving. Her remembering, and their letting her do so for them, was part of their relationship. This might not have been troublesome except for the contempt it could arouse in the woman and the resentment it caused in the men. While consciously she did the remembering out of love and a desire to care for them, some part of her disliked their inability to do so for themselves. This, too, boomeranged back on her: was her taking over the remembering causing them to stop doing so for themselves?

Her psychological axes were guilt, attachment and control. If she gave up remembering and doing, then she felt as though she had abandoned them and had left them unequipped. If she did remember for them, she felt on the edge of disdain for their unacknowledged dependency on her. Meanwhile, the contempt she emitted and the carping reminders to the men who were forgetting were deeply resented. The men felt controlled, pushed around, and 'forgot' even more, in passive rebellion. Of course, they remembered quite effortlessly in some areas. These were areas she had never penetrated, made her own. But in the ecology of the family system, as she strayed into an area, so the son or the father abdicated the remembering for himself.

When she abdicates the field of memory, the woman discovers that the men can indeed remember, though maybe not as she does. But in this declaration of separation, the emotional ecology of the family changes. She holds what is hers and stops intercepting what is theirs. The connections between them become less opaque, more direct and intelligible. She is unburdened of disdain and guilt, they of being accused of incompetence, of being controlled.

This seesaw of remembering and forgetting in the family environment echoes less benign conflicts between nations, groups of people or intimates. Conflictual forgetting is characterised by the kind of thing no one wants to remember. What we often call conscience is the part of us that can't forget but is conflicted about remembering. The conflicted memory gets detached from conscious experience to then become lodged in our memories as conscience.

Conscience is the part of the body politic, the couple, the family, that can't forget, that insists on being visible even if no one wishes to acknowledge its presence. It's valiant, incontestable, unremitting. It transforms the emotionally indigestible into a moral form. It's a crusade. But its tenacity is malleable: if the other or others remember, its persistence lessens, it can dissolve. It contests oblivion with knowledge, incorporation, owning, remembering. It gives way when it is recognised.

But remembering from the psychoanalytic perspective is not so much a moral issue as an interpersonal one and a collective contract. What's easily observed is that when more of us take responsibility for remembering what mustn't be forgotten, for acknowledging rather than denying, the less painful becomes the task of the rememberers. The less attractive, too, becomes the way of forgetfulness.

Men, Women, Boys, Girls

Fathers and Sons

A t the core of many a man's experience of himself is a void created by the absence of an emotionally vibrant relationship to his father. Paternity evokes a powerful image of responsibility taken on by a father towards his son.

This can involve a literal induction into the world of work, as in the passing on of particular skills – whether in farming, plastering, carpentry, learning the family business, or preserving inherited wealth. It can include sharing an interest in sports, literature, the pub and so on. Often, father-son contact is seen as an apprenticeship for a masculine life; the model for what is required of a man and how male-to-male relationships should be conducted. The hierarchy implicit within the father-son relationship seeps into much of masculine relating in which competition and positioning form a pole of male contact.

Part of the way in which boys become men is by adapting

and adopting a version of their perception of the authority, bearing and presence of their fathers, in the same way that a girl becomes a woman through absorbing aspects of her mother. However, for many men the closeness of the original maternal relationship sits in sharp distinction to the actual contact a boy has with his father. If a father enters into the child's view only occasionally, then the development of a masculine identity can feel like a leap into an unknown rather than the organic outcome of a close alliance.

Even today, where a great deal of thinking has come together acclaiming the value of active fathering, much fathering is hemmed in by the demands of jobs that keep men outside the domestic sphere or by habits and ideology that disdain their inclusion in the family as principals. Excluded from the ordinary business of the everyday by choice, circumstances or by default, fathering and masculinity is absorbed in a void. Fathers are often perceived as remote, absent or neglectful. We are not so very distant from the time when we simply expected them to bring in the money, carve the Sunday joint, be the final arbiter or authority a mother might invoke in order to discipline her child.

Direct emotional expression between fathers and sons was not highly touted as the way in which a boy would come to know his father or to know himself. A son who wanted more from his father may not have had a way to let him know this, to show him what he wanted or even to let himself realise what was missing.

A vague unease, emptiness and an inability to name what is wrong may mark a son's experience of his father, while feelings of confusion and a need to exert control may mark a father's relationship to his son. This hideously hurtful group of feelings, which makes for the fraught nature of the relationship between fathers and sons, was evident in the three men portrayed in Anna Raphael's Channel 4 film, *Men: From Here To Paternity*, in which three men from very different circumstances struggled to come to terms with the legacy of their fathers.

The Marquess of Bath, whose inheritance of privilege included a title, great wealth and an enormous estate, jostled with remaking his inheritance in his own counter-cultural image against the conventional expectations of his reactionary father, while at the same time encountering traditionalist values in his son and heir. Although a self-proclaimed libertarian, the Marquess's own fathering had left him with a softened but distinctly authoritarian relationship to his son. He wished to respect his son as he had wished for respect from his father. He wanted closeness but, nevertheless, the clash in temperament, sensibility and politics rendered this father-son relationship with a gaping hole; as portrayed in this film, it was characterised by misunderstanding and distance rather than by the closeness and regard both men desire.

Richard Olivier, the director, was struggling in the shadow of his father, Sir Laurence, the theatrical legend. We heard of his longing for a father who could show his love by putting him first, by making him as important as his career, by paying attention to what he needed as a child. But the father couldn't do this, and the son felt he was inadequate for not being able to hold his father's attention.

This feeling of not being enough for his father was reversed when Sir Laurence Olivier became physically frail and vulnerable. Then the father and son became close, as the father's need

propelled him towards his son. But the closeness was not satisfactory for Richard, burdened by his father's pain and sorrow.
His father was still both enigmatic and absent as a father for
him. While Richard melded together the images of Olivier's
heroic stage performances to fashion an image of a father to
hold on to, his paternal inheritance of enormous public fame
and acceptance clashed against his private anguish. Meanwhile
Richard was struggling to be a father to his own son, wanting to
offer him a more present and actively loving relationship than
the lacks he suffered with his own father.

Anna Raphael's third man, a young offender named Darren,
hoped to transcend the cycle of deprivation inherited from an
unknown father, whose career path was in crime. The birth of
his own son, while he was in detention, ignited his desire to be
a 'real father' to him. But when a father is literally absent, often
not even known, not spoken of with love or respect, there is an
even greater cavity.

Without the emotional link to a father even to fantasise about,
the inheritance involves fracture and loss. Men have made sense
of their maleness against the backdrop of their father and
through their work. Darren had grown up without a known
father and in appalling economic deprivation where jobs were
scarce. Where and how could he make sense of his masculinity,
a masculinity gutted of its conventional backbones? How could
such a boy become a man, and in whose image should he make
himself?

Darren had forged his identity through a perhaps unconscious alliance with the father's persona, that of criminalised
outsider. In his desire to form a good and active relationship to

his son, he had few positive supports and no personal internal imagery to draw on. The void that exists for him highlights the lacks that so many men experience in their struggle to develop a reliable and sustaining self-identity.

Loss, anger, violence, despair, distance, remoteness, unknowing and fear were the feelings conveyed by the men in Anna Raphael's film. These men were aware of what was missing. Their individual struggle – and that of many men today – is to reconstruct and rethink what is needed in the father-son relationship.

Mothers and Daughters

What's refreshing – at first – about Geri Halliwell's split from her Spice mates is the response in little girls who've been captivated by the band for the last year or two. They're interested all right, and discuss what they think has transpired between group members, but they aren't particularly dismayed.

Conflict between women, disagreements and fights, alarm girls less than we might have expected. They understand the Spice Girls' clashes with reference to their own lives: the squabbles in the playground, the individual versus the group, the wish to assert individuality.

It would be easy to be misled, to assume that the feelings of competition, of betrayal and abandonment which can impale women's friendships and work relationships – because they cause discomfort and guilt – were not going to trouble these little girls. It would be great to think that the hesitation so many women experience in showing disappointment or anger to friends no longer afflicts small girls. It would be great to think that girls who speak up, unafraid to express their views, were neither the exception nor the focus of others' envy. Certainly girls today seem able to voice opinions forcefully, tell each other where to get off, and to stand their ground.

Probe a little deeper, however, and we discover that despite the apparent ease with which girls assert themselves, the issues that beset their mothers remain complicated for them too.

To be sure, they seem more forthright in handling those difficult feelings which no longer need hiding. They can be openly angry, nasty and even thoughtless – something their mothers could never be. When they feel aggrieved they don't fret privately for days, or need to disgorge it immediately by discussing it with a friend, or stop their thoughts with guilt. They saunter in unfazed – or so it seems – with their dissension or aggression.

Ask a further question and we discover what's the same for them: 'It's stupid for Geri to fight and they should just get back together.' Splitting up is a bad thing. And there's the rub.

When it comes down to it, young girls don't find the spectre of differentiation much easier than their mothers. Girls still believe difference is threatening, that friendships can't sustain too much difference, that somewhere it is still too scary for girls to differentiate themselves from each other when they are close.

The sense that, if your friend doesn't like fruit you tell your mum that you don't either, is not something this generation of girls has escaped. The need to confirm identity by being the *same as* runs deep, raising worrying questions about the continuing fragility of a feminine identity. Many women still find it enormously hard to assert their voice in disagreement with one another – and if they do, they can think they have been very damaging. Feelings of envy and competition can easily be aroused between women, be experienced as frightening and potentially lethal to a relationship.

Until recently, girls' identity has been formed in the cradle of the mother–daughter relationship. The daughter is seen as the same as the mother in a way that is quite different from sons (who are regarded as different from the beginning). One difficulty mothers can experience, unconsciously, is this: they don't easily see their daughters as different from them. Without knowing it, they anticipate that their daughters will feel the same way about things as they do. As the most important person in their daughters' early life, they may frame their daughters' experience so that it conforms to their own. The daughter's separate experience may not be recognised and named, so that when she feels something different, she doesn't have anywhere to put it. It doesn't make emotional sense to her.

Still today, a common scene outside school in the morning involves mothers telling their daughters that they don't feel what they say they feel. If the girl expresses nervousness, she may still be chided for being silly; if you ask a girl a question about whether she likes something and she says she doesn't, you may still commonly hear her mother saying, 'Nonsense dear, why only last week you loved it.' The area of difference continues to be fraught for the mothers with their daughters.

The question it raises is whether there is still something threatening rather than simply habitual about this kind of exchange. And if it is threatening, why? Why is the different

experience of the other unwittingly denied? Why might a
mother seek confirmation for herself through her daughter's
assent? Why can't she easily see or tolerate a difference?

We know that for generations, women's experiences couldn't
be validated. What they saw, what they observed, what they felt,
was denied and distorted. And part – if only a small part – of
what made it possible for their experience not to be seen was the
way in which women managed what they did see internally.
Schooled from early on to deny their perceptions and desires,
they channelled energy into making things happen for others
and training themselves to see what others needed. Their identity would come through the relationships they made and
shaped – and in these relationships, the conformity they
expected from or foisted on their daughters was often critical.

Difference and separate desire, then, couldn't easily be managed. We adapted to patriarchy not through binding our feet
but through binding our minds and desires – and by enforcing
compliance on other women. We were all complicit and those
who broke the mould, speaking or acting differently, were
ostracised or envied. It was dangerous to be separate.

Now that women are visible in many different ways, there is
a chance to transform the psychology that went along with
patriarchy and made it possible. So it's good to see little girls
prepared to accept difference – and even aggression – without
finding it undermines their identity. But we can help them to
go further if we support their different points of view, hear
what their feelings are and don't subtly dissuade or recharac-
terise them. At the moment our 6- to 12-year-old girls are
ebullient. They've absorbed something wonderful about the
possibilities of femininity. They haven't yet learnt to shut down

and shut up as Carol Gilligan's latest research shows girls still do in adolescence.

Psychological change is slower than social change. What looks like progress, and is, can falter at crucial moments (at adolescence or, later, with motherhood) unless we underpin social change by enabling young girls and women to feel genuinely that they can act on desires. They can be separate and different without incurring the disapproval that silenced older generations.

Why Big Boys Don't Cry

The ongoing debate about men and masculinity has several distinct strains. In the cultural sphere, we have seen writers such as David Mamet railing against the perceived power of women to destroy them. In social policy, we have seen attempts to force absent fathers into a sense of economic responsibility.

And in the public sphere, commentators despair about hooliganism, unemployment and male violence. In these discussions, men are represented as either the hapless victims of societal changes or as an uncontainable wild force. Government pronouncements are all coded to appeal to the notion that men must behave like proper men, but this very notion of men appeals to the precise aspects of masculinity that cause such great distress.

What gets left out of these discussions is the way we bring up boys; what we expect of them and what we provide for them.

We act bewildered as the cute boys we cooed at in their prams transmogrify into the brutes on the terraces. We watch helpless as the little boys we cuddled find body contact through swiping one another in the playground or tackling each other in violent contact sports. So what is it that we are conveying about masculinity to boys? What are we valourising, what are we offering as points of identity for boys? What are we asking our boys to be?

Often without realising it, we are still raising boys to find and express themselves by standing alone, by knowing themselves through competing, by appearing strong. In contrast with girls, where relational and affiliative skills are stressed and an environment of connectedness and embeddedness with others and to others provides the context in which their lives are deemed to occur, we provide boys with a sense of self that exists not so much in connection but through a sense of separateness and of not needing.

In their passage from babyhood to boyhood, much effort is expended in helping little boys feel their power, strength and capability. We convey a sense that they can develop physical mastery.

Although some families may not conform to the following pattern, we breastfeed our boys past the time we breastfeed our girls; each feeding time is longer; we wean them more slowly; we potty train them later; and we hold them for longer periods of time. We use different tones of voice to soothe baby girls and baby boys, we use different language when we comfort them. The gender differences in the early physical handling of children have emotional parallels which are often difficult to spot.

While many parents will contest the idea that they treat children on gender lines, nevertheless we are all gendered beings and, whether purposefully or unconsciously, we will relate to baby girls and baby boys in a way that reflects our understanding and/or critique of gender.

The simplest illustration of this is to consider the fact that when we hear of a birth, the first question we ask after we know the baby and mother are well is its gender. If we don't know, we cannot proceed in the conversation. It is as though there is no such entity as a baby, only a baby boy or a baby girl. Without knowledge of its gender we don't know how to hold, see, or converse about the baby. Just try not finding out the sex of a baby and see how long you can hold out. It's impossible! From its earliest days we need to know its gender so that we can describe its activities to ourselves and each other and so we can introduce the baby to its world.

Of course, gender is not the only factor that influences how we see a baby. Its health is decisive. Its class, place in the family, race and ethnicity all determine the possibilities we see for it and how it will come to see itself.

But to return to the crucial nature of gender. When a child is gendered we can dress it, feed it, give it toys, talk to it and describe it. We will describe a boy as a robust eater, a girl as greedy; a boy as a terror, a girl as a tomboy. We will encourage certain characteristics in boys and others in girls, and although it is quite easy to see the gross differences in how we relate to children in terms of physical activities, it is less easy to be aware of the unconscious attitudes we transmit – the unconscious feelings we have about raising sons and raising daughters.

*

All these unconscious feelings join with our often unexamined attitudes about what boys and girls need to know or learn in order to become men and women who bear some resemblance to those categories. Panic about cross sexualities or oddball behaviour doesn't usually alarm parents or educators until early adolescence. We unconsciously act so congruently within gender that children who deviate are few and far between.

It is at the level of emotional relating where the most profound effects of gender can be seen, and it is at this level that the differences are, paradoxically, most hidden. We are often unaware of how we guide boys away from taking a certain kind of emotional responsibility for themselves, a responsibility that it is crucial for them to master if they are to find a masculinity that is more fulfilling and less precarious.

Whereas girls spend hours practising the emotional skills of looking after others, caring for them, nurturing them and processing their problems (all too often, it must be said, producing a constrained self-development), boys' energies are directed at mastering physical skills and suppressing their feelings. The crude characterisation, 'big boys don't cry', reflects a deeper, more persistent and subtler diversion of boys from their feelings. It isn't that boys don't have feelings, but they are rarely taught to name them, to understand their own or those of others. Most boys come to see non-heroic feelings as a distraction to be got rid of, rather than a vitalising part of themselves.

The feelings that do get practised endlessly are those of competition, of aggression, of ranking. Wrestling, fighting, following football scores or counting engine sizes on cars. Such feelings serve boys well for the world of competition, but help

them little when the structures that used to welcome them collapse, and fail them in terms of offering them an intimate
connection with self and others. The violence, aggression and
competition ruling boys' playgrounds offer them few forms of
expression for their confusions. When hurt, hit out; when vulnerable, be macho; when scared, hide it in bravado.

Our failure to let boys have a fuller emotional range sends
them down emotionally dead ends. They develop into men
who find it hard to recognise their feelings of vulnerability, fear,
tenderness, connection. And when they do experience these
feelings they are uneasy and try to soothe them by competing,
ranking and appearing not to need. Above all, they avoid taking
responsibility for such feelings by displacing them on to others
or acting them out aggressively.

The men around them fail to embody vulnerable feelings –
either representing a force or a pseudo strength. And as long as
the big boys don't cry, hurt or bleed, the little ones won't be able
to do it for long either, and our lovely little sons will be forced
to find emotional expression through the curtailment of their
tender selves.

The New Ugliness

A new word has broken through from psychological vocabulary: dysmorphia. We might as well get used to hearing about it and talking about it because, like its sister syndromes of anorexia nervosa and bulimia, it is a way of naming a set of feelings and practices that until recently were but a curiosity of the clinical life of psychotherapists and psychiatrists.

Like anorexia and bulimia, dysmorphia is a hatred of the self and a hatred of the body – a feeling of being overwhelmingly ugly. Like anorexia and bulimia, it mainly affects girls and women, and it is continuous with the kind of body preoccupation that we associate with femininity today. Although still relatively uncommon, dysmorphia holds up a mirror for us to understand something about almost every woman's (and, increasingly, man's) experience – the importance of our bodies and the insecurity around the way we look, present ourselves and are perceived.

In an image-led culture in which we seek to express our unique identity through our interpretation and integration of the possible images arrayed before us, the body has been used and viewed as the site where we inscribe who we are or who we wish to be taken as. Through how we dress, move and present ourselves, we signal each other on how we want to be perceived.

It is the prerogative of youth to overturn the codes of their elders. The easiest and most visible way in which this is done is through the transformation of an established sartorial standard. Adolescents contest what they experience as the suffocating confines of family and public space by dressing to offend, to demarcate, to disrupt and, above all, to announce their presence.

For nearly all of us the body is a canvas. We play with it and on it. We have the illusion that it is our creation. We believe we make it healthy or sick, fat or thin, beautiful or less beautiful by our attention to it. Our body is a personal object. If we fail to give it the right kind of attention, we are imperilled. As though it were Plasticine, we imagine that we can mould it and shape it if we only have the right amount of will. Attention to the body is the new morality: it is, we think, what we make it.

If we are ill, we are culpable. If we are fat, we are certainly culpable. (But for what exactly? What's the crime?) If we fail to find a way to express ourselves through our dress, our size, our appearance, we are somehow mutant. Surface is all.

The cruel fact is that most women want to change something about their bodies. They are dissatisfied, preoccupied, hypercritical. In extreme cases, such as in dysmorphia, the resculpting of the body and the attempted remaking of the face is a fight for life, for a place to feel good, or at least acceptable. Yet this goal is constantly and hurtfully elusive. The body is meant to cover up a profound interior upset, and it fails. It refuses the burden placed upon it. It confronts the individual with an immensity of self-loathing and disgust that can't be dammed up.

For a long time, psychoanalysts have thought of the body as a receptacle for those conflicts that can't be borne in the mind. Freud and Breuer's great work *Studies on Hysteria* tells of women with paralysed arms and legs for whose symptom no physical basis could be found. Anna O, who spoke in tongues and whose phantom pregnancy taught the two men the talking cure, demonstrated the ways in which painful thoughts and feelings which couldn't be spoken or thought about can be translated into bodily symptoms. For the century that has followed, psychoanalysis has split the mind and the body, seeing the body as a kind of sidekick, picking up the uncomfortable and unacceptable dramas of the soul. But now, with the rise in problems manifested on the body, new thinking is occurring; the idea that we have diseased minds and perfect bodies, or that our neurotic minds are encased in *un*neurotic bodies, no longer seems tenable. It is theoretical folly to think that if our minds, our psyches are hurting, then they can simply displace the hurt on to our bodies – this pristine bit of us that has no history, no hurt it bears.

The prevalence of eating problems, body image and body hatred problems has forced us to think of the body as having a psychological development which is parallel to but separate from that of the mind. The baby that takes in the idea that there is something wrong, something amiss with its desires and wants, that develops an insecurity about itself, is not simultaneously absorbing the idea that its body is safe and beautiful. Its bodily appetites can be responded to as inappropriately as its emotional needs, so that it develops a kind of body insecurity, rendering it vulnerable to trying to change its body to fit in with what is acceptable. We already know how damaging the preoccupation of image is for little girls whose transactions even in nursery school can be around clothes, fatness, thinness and prettiness.

In dysmorphia, this preoccupation is seeking a solution. The individual woman feels herself to be so ugly, the surface of her so unacceptable, that she has to efface it. She can't bear to be seen as she is, to expose the ugliness that she feels emanates from her; she feels malformed, monstrous, outside the range of acceptability. She paints away the face she has and tries to cover it with another. She may only go out at night in darkly lit places; she may be too distrusting to leave a small circle of friends and family.

The treatment of dysmorphia, like that of anorexia, involves accepting the individual's account of her ugliness, not dissuading her out of it with a more 'objective' account. It means understanding how ugly she feels and not cajoling. It means tolerating her pain rather than batting it away; being curious with her as to how she has come to feel this way about herself rather than telling her she's got it all wrong. In particular, it means finding a way for her to accept her perceived ugliness as a starting point to change. For the clinician, it means absorbing the ugliness into themselves, living with the pain of that experience and trying to understand it until what it involves becomes sufficiently comprehensible to dissolve and enable the individual to re-encounter herself and develop a more acceptable regard for herself, facially and emotionally.

When Sex is a Way to Love

I n the week before Jews all over the world mark Yom Kippur, the Day of Atonement – the time set aside to reflect on the past year – they think about the actions and thoughts that have been especially troublesome to them: occasions when they have acted at odds with their values, their conscience or their personal ideals. They scrutinise themselves for ways in which they have violated their personal notions of wrongdoing or when they have hurt others.

The process is essentially personal. It is not so much about an external view of transgression as it is a personal coming to terms with what has not sat right. The Day of Atonement signals a chance to make peace with what was wrong. This is done not by being forgiven but by finding a way to accept inside of oneself the rather more difficult idea that one is capable of doing wrong, of inflicting hurt, of being cruel.

When that idea can be grasped, one can then begin the process of taking responsibility for one's actions and explore the complexities of what motivated one's cruelty, deceit, or neglect.

The spiritual dimension of this annual confrontation with self has something akin to the therapeutic process. Therapy is often characterised, or perhaps I should say caricatured, as the place in which an individual goes to blame someone else – usually a parent – for the harm they have caused. But while from time to time an individual may find it useful to locate culpability for their difficulties outside themselves, more important and profound aspects of the therapy process centre on assessing the situation an individual has found her or himself in and how, given those circumstances, they have then construed them.

Therapy taps into a very painful dimension of experience. It enables a person to think about the ways in which they may have unwittingly contributed to their own pain and distress and that of others. It looks at how someone can come to inflict pain and hurt on others; how and why acts of cruelty are enacted against others as well as against oneself. Therapy seeks to create a space between actions and feelings so that difficult feelings can be pondered over, even accepted inside oneself, without having to be immediately denied, expelled or turned against oneself.

For example, in therapy with an individual engaged in the relentless sexual pursuit of others who has deceived himself or his friends and family and who, cornered, now feels bad and is trying to change his behaviour, we would not so much be looking for relief in the form of repentance as Clinton has done, but trying to understand why they felt compelled to engage with others in this way.

Psychoanalytic understandings echo those of the historians. If we fail to understand, then we are compelled to repeat. Atonement, forgiveness, repentance are recast in the therapy process. The forgiving comes not from some external source but the capacity to understand, and out of that understanding to find within some compassion towards oneself which breaks the repetitive cycle of transgression and repentance.

It could be argued that a compulsive fornicator has already forgiven himself or feels no need to do so; that the repetitive nature of the act implies in itself an ability to too easily excuse and forgive, as well as exposing a callous disregard for others. But that would be to take the surface for the depth and the action for the totality. Strange as it may seem, the individual caught up in repetitively damaging behaviour which they are unable to acknowledge as serious is often plagued not by an overcapacity to forgive themselves but by an inability to stand the extreme anxiety and pain that leads them to unceasingly pursue others as a form of relief from their own distress. Indeed, the repetitive behaviour may work well enough to cover up and protect the individual from knowing much about what motivates or stimulates their behaviour.

It may be that a man drawn to flirt with and sexually conquer many of the women he encounters is driven not by some furious sexual appetite, not even opportunism, but by an inability to register a deep distress in himself. He flirts and needs to seduce another because it assuages a set of feelings he has no way to acknowledge.

He craves acceptance, a sense of being needed, wanted and desired because it soothes and temporarily answers a need he knows no other way to address. By fashioning that need in a sexual idiom he bypasses difficult questions and feelings that might otherwise overwhelm him: questions as to why he feels so insatiable that he has constantly to be gratified, so unlovable that he needs repeated confirmation of his desirability, so unrecognised that he must always be in others' thoughts.

Although such a man's behaviour can be extremely destructive and hurtful to others, it may seem less so to him. It answers a habitual hunger. As long as that behaviour is available it may cause little conflict inside him. It is only when it is no longer available or viable that a gap opens and the man is confronted with the feelings that lie behind his behaviour. It is then that catastrophic feelings – of extreme emptiness, anxiety, disintegrating and of rampant self-hatred – appear, which can be so powerful that they are experienced as annihilating. Now he suffers unbearably. He doesn't know what to do with himself, for his avenue for distancing himself and displacing those feelings – perhaps by exploiting others in his pursuit of temporary relief – has evaporated. Whatever good feelings he has been able to collect for himself are negated under the weight of fear and negativity.

In therapy the task is to help the person with the onslaught of painful attacks which emanate from their inner world. To find a way through, so that they neither offload what they experience on to others nor accept the feelings as the summation of what they are. The process is geared rather to an acceptance and understanding of the psychological states that caused the pain and a way to find a certain compassion towards oneself. It is the compassion that creates the conditions which make different choices possible. When that compassion can be felt, the individual reaches a different level of feeling about himself, a kind of grief for the experience of life as he has known it.

This grief is the beginning of a reconciliation with oneself which is based not on forgiveness but a kind of humility: of understanding the limitations and options one had available. These options may have rested on a desire to deny or escape from the indignity of the pain one suffered and so it became recast. The self-hating man may have recast himself as a lover, for in that image he could find some aspect of himself that expressed what he wished he could do – to love and be loved.

Forgiveness and atonement are complicated processes. They aren't so easily given by others but rather they must be fought for within oneself. To begin to grieve for one's misdemeanours, for the hurts one has caused, is to grieve too for the paucity of resources one has had to manage life with, and finally to accept that those impoverishments cannot be overcome by defiance and salves – but through engagement with them.

The Other Side of Caring

The bitch is the woman few of us wish to be. Nasty and spiteful, in extremis malevolent, selfish and self-involved, the bitch is a category into which we collect disparate types of behaviour by women which we find hurtful, perplexing, mean, self-centred or aggressive. In one way, the bitch is an affront to our sense of what a woman should be. In another she is an expectable aspect of all women: wily, devious or nasty. She is a counterpoint to the female who is sought for her nurturing kindness.

Entwined in the notion of bitch are many meanings. There is the competitive woman, the devious woman or the selfish woman intent on self-promotion whatever the cost. Without wishing to rehabilitate the term, I am intrigued by the ease with which we use this shorthand to describe all manner of women's transgressions. But what are we really responding to when we call someone a bitch? And what is bitchy behaviour?

The bitch acts as she is not supposed to do, promoting self-interest, apparently untouched by the disapproval her actions arouse. In some instances, her seeming imperviousness to criticism and social approbation stirs admiration. The bitch transgresses social norms. At other times, her behaviour enrages and confuses – so that our response is not only 'how can she be like that?', but 'how dare she break the rules?'

The girdle around acceptable female behaviour is so taut that when it over-stretches, the woman is described as an outcast. The bitch is the opposite of a nice girl. The bitch's violation highlights the constraints on women's behaviour and emotional expression. Certain types of behaviour and expression are reinforced, while others are abhorred. A divide is created between women whose behaviour is acceptable and those whose behaviour is not.

Women can be demarcated and threatened by the label of the bitch. The notion of the bitch is in conflict with the more generous ways in which we see women – as caring and nurturing. But are these two ways of being exclusive, or do they perhaps need one another as a result of the imperatives that women are subjected to?

The imperative of caring and nurture – of being on alert to attend to the wishes and needs of others, to foster, soothe, understand, facilitate and hearten others – is an important and deeply valuable aspect of anyone's emotional repertoire. The relational bonds women typically make and keep going are crucial to well-being. A woman's capacity to behave in such a way contributes to her feelings of self-worth and competence. They are not overlays on her personality but ingrained, and therefore central attitudes and responses she has developed from childhood.

They are so intrinsic that they feel immutable, and when they are challenged or when a woman feels unable to call upon the caring, nurturing aspects of herself, she may feel bereft of an essential piece of her identity. But this identity is honed at great cost. For the other side of caring and nurturing is that it can exclude the pursuit of personal goals – goals which conflict with the need always to have others in view.

In the past 20 years, women's dissatisfaction with the social and emotional requirement that they be midwives to the needs and activities of others has meant that they have contested not just the economic and social arrangements but the emotional arrangements, too, inside themselves, between women and between sexes.

In the unravelling of the emotional arrangements, women who attempt to pursue their own goals, who break the ties of female camaraderie by being loners, or who try to rewrite the social and emotional contract between women, arouse envy, jealousy, anger and alarm in other women. The bitch is one expression of women's attempt to get out from under the emotional contract. It may be a particularly uneuphonic one, but its very unattractiveness derives from the searingly difficult break the woman may be making with her caring and nurturing side.

In trying to set those aside, she may have little experience of self-assertion. Her determination, but lack of practice about pursuing what she wants, may render her behaviour ugly; so that while it may not be malevolent, it appears so because it inelegantly defies acceptable female behaviour.

Of course, female self-assertion is a tricky business. Not only can it arouse envy and fear in other women, it can feel threatening to the woman herself who, in daring to place herself and her desires on the table, fears she may lose a sense of self which has depended upon her capacity to be warm and caring. It can feel as if she has broken a taboo and imperilled her identity. She has cast herself out of the lot of women into a no-person's land where her behaviour and emotional responses seem alien.

So if we peel away the label of the bitch and endeavour to understand what is encoded within the apparently offensive behaviour, we may see that it is not so much full of spite and malevolence as a sign of both a collective fear about the woman intent on pursuing her own goals and an awkwardness arising from the guilt and conflict she has about doing so. It can feel so difficult to disentangle oneself from the expectations and the internal restraints on self-expression that assertion can feel murderous and dangerous.

The difficulties are amplified by women's disownership of aspects of self which are then projected on to other women. So one woman's difficulties with her own power and desires may find expression in the criticism of another who has been able to activate hers. The despair the first woman feels about not being able to actuate her own desires are temporarily soothed when her emotional energy is engaged in the envy of the other; she can unload her own distress by being critical.

So the bitch and the nice girl are not so much contradictory formulations of femininity as complementary ones. As long as women are prevented by social mores and internal psychological proscriptions from legitimately pursuing their own desires, they'll do so in ways that are either circuitous – earning the characterisation manipulative – or in ways that embody a fierce attempt to counteract the guilt and conflict which acting for themselves engenders within them.

Bitches may be deeply unpleasant, but the feelings they arouse can tell us about the level of personal desire that is being repressed.

SECTION V

Therapy

Couched in Myth

One way and another, there's invariably quite a lot in the
newspapers about psychotherapy and psychoanalysis.
Descriptions of the craft depict silver-tongued Svengalis enticing
the vulnerable, acting as advisers, using them as mouthpieces for
their own ideas. These parodies of the purposes and nature of
therapy have captured the public imagination, leaving therapists and those who consult them bewildered by accounts at
such a great distance from their experience. Such is the scorn,
confusion, ridicule and fear surrounding discussion of psychotherapy and psychoanalysis, that little written is accurate.

Of course, the distortions cannot all be laid at the hands of
the media. There has been both conflict and unease in the pro-
fession about a wide dissemination of its work, which adds to
the mystery and confusion. Psychoanalytic practice has roots in
neurology, psychiatry, psychology and philosophy, but a home

in none of them. While its ways of seeing contribute to many disciplines today, and applied psychotherapy makes it possible for our emergency services to function, clinical work is still an enigma to many who have little to draw on apart from Hollywood or Woody Allen caricatures. And so into the void enter a host of fantasies and projections. The content of most of these can be rendered as follows: the therapist unduly influences the vulnerable analysand. The source of the undue influence is the power relationship – the fact that a distressed person is forced to trust another in a time of trouble and is then, inevitably, exploited.

Need, trust and exploitation are in fact at the very heart of psychoanalysis. They are part of what brings people to therapy. A person's needs – whether denied, hidden from view, distorted or unmet – are part of what is explored within therapy. Similarly, the ability to trust is not taken for granted. Rather, the therapy becomes a setting in which possible difficulties around trusting can be looked at. Exploitation – the feeling of being used, of one's interests being subverted by those of the therapist (or anyone else) – forms part of the therapy conversation. No therapist worth their salt conducts an analysis or a therapy without scrupulous regard to these issues. The charges laid at the psychoanalysist's door are curious because they conform not, I believe, to psychoanalysis's failings but to its strengths.

It is hard to right these misperceptions in one article, but it is possible to give a flavour of the processes of psychotherapy which can perhaps correct some of the distortions that characterise its descriptions in the press.

First, what it isn't. It isn't a vehicle for the transferring of ideas from the therapist into the mind of the analysand. The patient or client is not a receptacle, who, having emptied their minds of dark thoughts and emoted their way through them, then exchanges these thoughts for others that the analyst provides. Nor is it a way to boost 'self-esteem'. Self-regard comes from understanding and accepting self. This process, if derailed in childhood, requires considerably more than the injection of any soothing balm.

Second, it isn't about bolstering people up by uncritically assenting to their point of view and by providing a special kind of supercharged friendship. Psychotherapy involves recognising the situation in which a person finds her or himself, then holding still for long enough to think with them about their circumstances. It is about finding a way to enable the person to see what may be their own contribution to their predicament, so they can be mindful of any possible unconscious motivation or collusion on their part.

Third, psychotherapy is not about making people dependent. Human beings are dependent on one another; we need each other to survive. Our sense of autonomy only evolves in the context of meaningful and sustaining connection to others. For many in therapy, it is the impediments against dependency, the fears that surround what it means to become attached to another and others, that require addressing. Therapy doesn't create the conditions of dependency, although it may highlight a person's relationship to it. Therapy is the work of trying to understand what is going on when dependency and autonomy cannot easily be achieved, and when a person disdains their own or the other's needs for connection.

Now to some of what the therapist is aiming to do within the

relationship. I say some of because, like all relationships, each
therapy relationship (while sharing commonalities) is unique.
The feelings, concerns and preoccupations of the individual,
and the responses aroused by her or him in the therapist, will set
an idiosyncratic tone and texture to the sessions.

First, of course, the therapist listens and engages, paying
attention to what the person says and how they say it, and the
feelings, body movements, hesitations surrounding what is and
isn't said. The therapist hears and absorbs uncritically what is
being voiced. In the listening, the therapist is finding his or her
way into entering their patient's or client's experience. They try
to experience how life feels from the inside for the person, so
that they can begin to comprehend the hows and whys of their
patient's or client's particular knots, difficulties, hurts, disappointments and passionate pulls.

Alongside hearing, absorbing and entering into the emotional world of another, the therapist endeavours to make
meanings about their situation with their patient or client. This
is what is conventionally termed interpreting, and where many
of the confusions and myths surrounding psychoanalysis occur.
The patient speaks, the doctor interprets. But I see what happens between the two people engaged in therapy as a
conversation. The therapist may tentatively offer a perspective
to be considered by the two of them. This may be modified,
rejected, elaborated and so on. But it is together that meaning
is constructed and new ways of understanding come that provide for an emotional settling inside the analysand. As
something is understood afresh, different possibilities are
opened up.

*

In short, psychoanalysis is very far along from its cartoon image: the analyst interprets, the patient agrees and, therefore, the interpretation is correct. The analyst interprets, the patient disagrees and, therefore, the interpretation is even more correct.

An additional way in which the therapy process conveys the emotional world of the other is by the therapy relationship becoming a stage for a playing out of the very issues that concern the person. The analysand unconsciously authors a script which is dramatised in the therapy as the therapist discovers herself or himself inclined to take on an unfamiliar role. Through the enactment, which the therapist both observes and emotionally surrenders to inside her or himself, the power of what troubles the patient or client is felt, with the possibility then of being understood.

These aspects of therapy – hearing, absorbing, thinking, entering and re-enacting – are combined rather than sequential. The prominence of each aspect depends upon the individuals engaged. But these are the processes that can be observed by clinicians who engage in the psychoanalytic enterprise. Their aim, of course, lies in Freud's most eloquent aphorism: psychoanalysis as a clinical practice is about transforming hysteria into ordinary human misery.

The Political Psyche

Politics and psychoanalysis have often been seen as strange
bedfellows, but at various points in the life of the relatively
new discipline of psychoanalysis, there have been flirtations
between these two ways of explaining the individual and their
place in the world.

For the British, the home-grown Laingian assault on conventional psychiatry nearly 30 years ago presented a liberating
view on sanity and insanity, by looking at the generally mad
way we organise so much of our society.

From Laing, his associates and those whom his work
inspired, came new ways of practising psychotherapy. The radical climate of the Sixties and Seventies led to a reassessment of
all the institutions intersecting with daily life, including critiques of orthodox therapy. But this climate didn't simply
abandon psychological insight, it sought to radicalise and

broaden it; to include a psychological understanding of the inter-relationship between the individual, family and political structures.

Elsewhere in Europe, psychoanalysis became part of the legacy of the political movements of 1968. Dutch women set up an elaborate network for self-help therapy groups; the Italians reversed their policy on the hospitalisation of mental patients; German radicals looked at the psycho-politics of National Socialism and its aftermath; and, in Paris, the Lacanian psychoanalytic seminar became a happening – a gathering of critical perspectives on the status quo.

Meanwhile, on the other side of the Atlantic, a radical therapy movement – aiming to free people from mental institutions; to stop psychiatric abuse in prisons; to question what was sane and what was healthy, and to expose the work of the so-called soft cops (welfare workers, teachers, psychologists) who policed the populace with kid gloves by resocialising their desires back into socially acceptable norms – unleashed an energy which reframed canonical psychoanalysis. Homosexuality was no longer seen as deviant; women's psychology was on the agenda, the class and racial biases encoded in therapeutic practice began to be exposed.

But the energy of the Sixties and Seventies gave way to a decade of public reaction. The beginnings of the productive liaison between psychoanalysis and politics continued, but in unexpected ways. Childhood sexual abuse was (re)discovered. New psychological symptoms such as eating problems, came to the fore, masculinity began to be problematised, and so on. Although novel institutions and new ways of understanding and working with distress still evolved, much of psychotherapy and psychoanalysis returned to its relatively comfortable ensconcement in establishment institutions, where their insights were tolerated, and where their capacity to resocialise dissident strains was sometimes in evidence.

Many formerly politically radical people, stranded by events, were drawn into psychotherapy and psychoanalysis in their quest to cope with new social forces and understand themselves better.

The ideology of the Eighties, with its eulogisation of the individual and the promotion of a nineteenth-century Samuel Smiles type of self-help, dovetailed with the more conformist aspects of psychotherapy and psychoanalysis. Individuals in difficulties were encouraged to see their distress as, in some sense, self-generated, with the resulting confusion between the need to take responsibility for one's emotional state and a practice of self-blame. Psychic disquiet was divorced from its relational and political cultural context. And, apart from feminism, politics severed itself from understanding the personal and psychological.

This cleavage was a disservice to psychoanalysis; a disservice to politics, and a disservice to individuals or families seeking help. There is a fine line between personalising the routes of distress, of alienation and disjuncture, and locating those routes, that alienation, that disjuncture solely within the individual. Instead of the creative tension implicit in the phrase 'the personal is political', the personal became a person falsely denuded of the political.

Of course, we must specify and investigate how and why individuals experience and act upon their upset. The particulars of experience are part of what makes us human, and in psychotherapy it is the particulars of individuals' experience that are explored. People do not come to therapy seeking relief from a malaise that they would describe as induced by political arrangements. The economically dependent women in an unhappy marriage may seek therapeutic help to ease her situation. She may want to find ways to stay in the marriage and transform it, or she may want to find ways to leave. Her history, her initial attraction to her husband, her feelings of loyalty, her anger about what she is not getting or feels unable to give, her conflicts about what she is entitled to expect, the possible parallel of her marriage with that of her parents', her difficulties with her desires, are all thought about in good therapy.

In the course of her exploration of personal difficulties, this same woman will organically situate her dilemmas within a context that refers to the contemporary sexual politics of marriage: the meaning of heterosexual relationships, the imbalance in the emotional exchange between women and men, and so on.

The complete interpretation in therapy has to allow for a link between dimensions of experience that are particular to her, but which also connect her experience with the social and political arrangements that have contributed to her becoming who she is, participating as she does, seeing herself as able to act or not act, so that she has a chance to try out the emotional possibilities she wants for herself, cognisant of her personal situation.

The personal and the political – two modes of understanding – require each other. We need both. We can't understand ourselves in isolation, nor can we explain power arrangements without reference to the personal and emotional meanings that keep our political arrangements in place.

As psychotherapeutic understandings once again reach outside the consulting room door, we can pick up and enhance the project that has mostly been underground this past decade. We can continue our exploration of the political psyche.

Prozac

T hrough an amusing if broad piece of symbolism in the
Everyman film, *Welcome To Happy Valley* (1994) we see
the large, rosy-red, regulation-size apples from the orchards of
Wenatchee, Washington State, being sprayed, washed off,
shined up and packed in boxes just as the formerly depressed
but now comfortingly content patients of psychologist Jim
Goodwin are doused with the synthetic happiness of Prozac,
the pharmaceutical industry's most recently successful anti-
depressant.

The analogy between the intensive chemical treatment of
apples and the 700 formerly depressed citizens of the Prozac
capital of the world is chilling. Undoubtedly, there are people
for whom a chemical correction is helpful and humane on a
short-term basis. The capacity to think, feel and see their way
through extreme grief, despair or trauma is impaired and they

feel enabled by the relief that this latest anti-depressant can
provide. Life becomes liveable and possible and their adaptation
to the drug is unproblematic. However, Prozac is an old story
with a new twist. It is the latest in a very worrying production
line of chemical cocktails that modify and disrupt synaptic and
neurotransmitter patterns. Prozac is a very successful drug.
While manufacturer Eli Lilly closely guards information about
its usage and profitability, a very low estimate puts 17 million
North Americans on the drug annually and increasing numbers
of children.

The twist with Prozac was the canny marketing which elevated its status to that of a pleasurable designer or recreational
drug which is just so good at making one feel better, enhancing
reality, chilled out, and non-confrontational. The drug has been
likened to corrective lenses, it lets you see more comfortably and
better. This line has exempted it from the kind of criticism or at
least healthy scepticism we ought to have routinely when any
drug comes on the market. Certainly the experience of Valium
users and the devastation wrought in some clinical trials of
Halcyon should alert us to potential problems in the widespread uptake of this drug and lead us to question its clean
image – an image that means that it is being prescribed to 6-
and 7-year-olds diagnosed as depressed as well as to pregnant
women.

Several years ago, I gave a paper at a conference in the West
Country which had received a contribution from Eli Lilly.
Although it isn't unusual to find pharmaceutical companies at
medical conferences, what did strike me about this particular
campaign was the paint-by-numbers pads we were given to
help us diagnose our patients. On the first page were questions

drawn from anxiety and depression scales that we should direct towards our patients. Have you been worrying a lot? Have you been irritable? Have you had a difficult time relaxing? Have you had low energy? Have you had a loss of interests? Have you lost confidence in yourself? Have you felt hopeless? If the hapless patient answered yes to two or more questions then the physician was to turn over the page to discover the next set of questions which related to sleeping difficulties, waking early, poor appetite and so on. Some positive answers here and Prozac is indicated.

Aside from the standard fare of tissue boxes, pads and pens that were being given out, a well-produced booklet on depression directed at physicians was on offer. Purporting to be a balanced, objective view on depression – its history, causes, social-class spread, age and gender breakdown – the booklet looked as though it had been produced by the Department of Health and even had a Whitehall address. But this was not produced by the Civil Service or even a quango, but by the Office of Health Economics, an organisation founded (and one presumed funded) by the Association of the British Pharmaceutical Industry.

The booklet discusses the economic aspects of depression relative to the NHS, and suggests the efficacy of a combined pharmaceutical and cognitive behavioural therapeutic intervention which depends on 'changing certain ways of thinking'. The thrust is not to alter circumstances but 'to adjust the way the person perceives and reacts to existing situations'. And herein lies an agenda which those concerned with mental health issues must address. Clinical depression is deeply debilitating. It does mean that one perceives the world as a menacing or foreboding place; that one's experience of one's ability to act to change one's circumstances is circumscribed and that despair tinges experience so that life can look very blocked indeed. Clinical depression is a frightening place to be in and the GP who encounters it is under pressure to prescribe. He or she is too short of time to bring to bear whatever psychiatric skills are needed in the confines of a 10-minute consultation. The temptation to offer the patient medication, which might provide a cushion against their depression, hurt and despondency, may be compelling. But prescribing in the first or even second instance, in the face of what gets lumped together as depression, is yet another expression of the emotional illiteracy that pervades our society. It is telling us that pain can't be borne, lived through and tolerated by either depressed people or those around them.

Where earlier anti-depressant drugs produced a cotton-wool effect, numbing the pain of people whose social and or personal circumstances rendered them relatively helpless, Prozac and the other SSRI (selective serotonin re-uptake inhibitors) drugs are favoured for their supposed feel-good qualities and the adjustment they allow the individual to make to their circumstances. This rendering of feelings means that, in effect, we are saying that loss doesn't need to be felt, confusion sorted through, grief digested, depression understood. There are plenty of stories about the normal trauma of everyday life being transposed into the trauma of prescription drug-taking. Yet it is our responses to adverse circumstances that make us human, and our capacity to survive these feelings and grow through and from them is part of what constitutes maturity.

Lest people who have been helped by prescription drugs

misread me, I'm not arguing that we should enter into a mass orgy of painful feelings or that we should banish tricyclics or SSRIs. Genuine relief from pain is important, and psychotropic drugs judiciously prescribed have a significant place in medicine and psychotherapy. But I am concerned about the routine administering of anti-depressants which may rob a person of their capacity to feel that they can function without them.

We need to ensure that the prescriber is seeking to help to heal the patient rather than collude with those aspects of our culture which find painful feelings terrifying and unmanageable. When drugs are prescribed out of this motivation, a long-term dependency can ensure. We must remember that coming off any psychotropic drug causes physical as well as psychological disruption.

Psychic pain is excruciating. Prolonged depression is debilitating and damaging. Medication can be helpful in the short term, and in a limited number of cases for longer. But we need to direct our attention to alternative methods to work through depressions and come out the other side of them – such as speaking with a vicar, a friend, a professionally trained counsellor, psychotherapist or support group. Depression muffles our mind and spirit. medication used on a permanent basis, proposed as a solution, becomes part of the problem. We need to address bigger questions. What is so terribly wrong with our world that so many psychotropic drugs are produced and used daily? Doesn't this suggest we need to reorganise our lives to produce less depression rather than manufacture more drugs to combat it?

Beware the Prejudiced Analyst

You are well regarded, have a loving, stable relationship, an interesting job, good enough housing and a circle of friends. But . . .

Inside you, things don't seem to fit together properly. You aren't all of a piece. A painful hole sits at your centre. Something is wrong. At times you feel fraudulent, as though you don't have a right to your good relationship. Sometimes, you test it almost to the limit. At work, you exude a certain competence, but inside you worry and fret: can I really do this? How long before they find out I'm a fake?

You feel as though you exist in compartments. Some parts of you are lively, giving and engaged. Other parts feel fraudulent, motivated by personal insecurity. You find yourself taking on challenges almost as a way of life – just to prove to yourself that you're OK. You are invigorated while you are on the climb, and life seems full of hope. But the resulting successes don't make you feel better for very long. Worse still, they can reinforce the sense that you've got away with something. Like Groucho Marx, you can't allow yourself anything but contempt for any club that will let you join.

Your different self-perceptions can coexist, but it is painful. You lose a certain self-assurance. When your confidence is crowded out by self-doubt, you wonder why you are so psychically dishevelled. Not knowing how to deal (on your own or with your loved ones) with this disjuncture at the heart of you, you decide to go for psychotherapy. Friends have found it more or less useful.

Psychotherapy has become more readily available in the UK since you've been an adult, and the stigma around entering therapy or analysis has abated. Having read around the field a bit and found psychoanalytic ideas engaging, you ask around for names. You're nervous, but in an excited sort of way.

There's just one snag, one little wrinkle: you are homosexual. You've been gay ever since you could think about the idea. Although it's been a source of confusion, especially when you were an adolescent, for years it hasn't been a fundamental problem. It doesn't feel as if that's the issue. Of course, you've suffered discrimination. you've gone through the struggle to come out and the confrontation with your own internal homophobia. You had a partner in the past who was not able to come out and that caused friction and pain in your relationship, even though it wasn't that uncommon a scenario in your network. Relatively secure in your sexual identity, you want help for the psychological compartmentalising that constrains your happiness.

The snag is that much of British psychoanalytic training and teaching is retrograde about sexuality. At the heart of the psychoanalytic endeavour there is a contradiction. A discipline that prides itself on its capacity to question, to pursue the idea behind the idea, to be curious rather than censorious, to acknowledge the transgressive and socially inconvenient, finds itself rigid in its understanding of the development of sexual orientation. While the psychoanalytic relationship is in principle a place of discovery, this discovery can be clipped by the heterosexual orthodoxies.

Heterosexuality, while not necessarily normative for Freud, has become normative for many of the psychoanalytic institutes in the United Kingdom where the construction of heterosexuality is not questioned but taken as given. Homosexuality, by contrast, is viewed largely as a perversion.

That such ideas are fostered in training worries a significant group of psychoanalytic psychotherapists, who were alarmed by the arguments which for 30 years Charles W. Socarides, the psychiatrist and psycho-analyst, has been promoting: the position that homosexuality is a perversion.

He believes that homosexuality can (and should) be cured. For him homosexuality operates against the cohesive elements in society. He sees a great political threat from homosexuals as a grouping, and writes as though they were the dominant force in the culture rather than an embattled and discriminated-against minority: 'The forces allied against heterosexuality are formidable and unrelenting.'

We have here the personal prejudices of a practising analyst masquerading as fact and theory. Socarides's son, Richard, the high-level Clinton appointee who happens to be gay, is forever running into colleagues in the gay community who were sent by their parents to his father to be (unsuccessfully) straightened out. Socarides senior is not simply describing how he understands the development of sexual orientation. He is on a mission; his professional life has focused on the treatment and cure of homosexuality.

The controversy stirred up by a recent visit allows us to confront and dismantle prejudice.

In the meantime, our imaginary potential analysand must sort through the quagmire of his or her emotional life deprived of the guarantee that his or her exploration of self will be untainted by a psychotherapeutic orthodoxy long abandoned in the United States. Although many enlightened psychotherapists will give consideration to the individual's issues without defining them in terms of their sexual orientation, this should by no means be taken for granted. Without this guarantee, it is hard for an analysand in therapy to look safely at whatever version of homophobia he may have internalised. He has no reassurance that his therapist has explored his own. Indeed, he would have every reason to expect potential prejudice.

At a time when the Institutes which provide the bulk of training for NHS psychotherapists and analysts are under considerable pressure to rethink their admission procedures re homosexual candidates, Socarides' teachings give entirely the wrong signal. What needs supporting are challenges to these ideas and the delivery of unprejudiced mental health services.

Grown-up
Vulnerabilities

For a decade or so now, metaphors such as the 'inner child', 'the baby within' or 'the little girl inside' have entered our vocabularies. People use such phrases to render comprehensible some of the disjunction in their emotional lives. In doing so, 'the inner child' is elevated as the innocent, the bearer of truth, the essence of who we are. This of course jars with our cultural propensity to designate certain emotional states as childish, as ways of being we should have left behind. In this sensibility, we use the terms childish and emotional as an act of censure and reprobation.

There is a tension between these two different appropriations of 'the child'. In the latest chronicle of our lost selves and the attempt to link up with repressed emotional experiences, we use words like 'the little girl' or 'the child within' to describe what may be an accurate cleavage between rational and predictable ways of being and the often impetuous and urgent eruption of emotional states. But a descriptive truth which divides a person up into an inner child and an adult self unwittingly perpetuates and invigorates a split between different aspects of mental functioning, hence different aspects of our selves. It makes the integration of those 'inner child' aspects *less* rather than more likely.

Of course, we are often inclined to label confusing, annoying or inconvenient emotional states as belonging to our child self. In searching for a language to describe private experience, particularly when we feel vulnerable, shy or bereft of a place to put what we are feeling, we may stretch out to use metaphors of childhood or babyhood when an emotional life was at least expected. Paradoxically, although much of childhood development involves learning to fit our emotional responses into what is acceptable socially and in our families – so that growing up involves the suppression of certain kinds of expression and some inevitable repression – we can romanticise the experience of childhood, remembering in it the space available to feel a wide range of emotional responses, as though there is a time in childhood that is 'before the fall'.

Psychoanalytic theory unintentionally compounds this popular elevation of childhood to a precious or protected space. A therapy narrative often drifts back towards a period when a particular feeling or memory froze in time, clipping from that point on the free and easy expression or feeling of certain emotional states. The memories act as a template for the adult disposition of emotional states and possibilities. But this formulation that we all tend towards is itself a construction and a bit fantastical. What we remember in those memories is not the moment when free expression was limited, but the moment when the constraints we were already operating within either became obvious to us or were channelled in specific ways.

Childhood innocence is a myth. Few of us had perfect childhoods or childhoods in which the subtlety and range of emotional expression was encouraged inside and outside the home. From our entry into the world to our starting at school, our emotional life was shaped in interaction with those around us. However broad-minded and emotionally literate our families of origin, certain emotional expression would have been welcomed, some discouraged. In the making of ourselves into who we are, we found the parts of ourselves that could be acknowledged by others. In their recognition of the parts of us that they could receive, we found ourselves. As our lives broadened outside the family and the carers of early childhood, we showed, and experimented with showing, aspects of self that may not have been welcomed at home. And if we did so with ease, we in turn received recognition for those aspects of self which became integrated into our personalities. However fortunate we were, though, certain emotional (and intellectual, physical, sexual) possibilities would have been closed to us and others open. If psychoanalysis has anything to tell us, it is about the intransigence of early influence and the power of early parental and family relationships to shape self-experience.

The frozen memory then captures not the moment when emotional life stopped, but when we learnt consciously – as opposed to absorbed unconsciously – the emotional frame in which we could conduct ourselves. The shock of that confrontation is often what fuels the specific memory: we became aware.

It is this awareness – the time when we become cognisant – that makes the metaphor of the inner child so handy. It fits with experience and explains in a simple phrase those aspects of self that have become semi-detached. The so-called inner child is no more real, valid or authentic than any other aspect of self. It may contain within it, however, sets of emotional tableaux that are either undeveloped or feelings that are hard to integrate.

When we characterise certain feelings as pertaining to our inner child, we create a kind of space which may allow us to explore feelings that we would otherwise disregard. But if we ennoble the state of inner child at the expense of the adult, we do ourselves a great disservice. We fail to integrate a whole range of emotional states into our adult personae, ironically perpetuating that which we wish to contest. The 'inner child' slips into being the container for the emotional states the adult cannot acknowledge and embrace within his or her adult self.

The 'inner child' metaphors can be of more than descriptive value. They can be a bridge to welcoming into adulthood those difficult experiences that make us petulant, vulnerable, and so on. Instead of hiving those responses off as the expression of our 'inner child', we can recognise that as adults we are often susceptible to painful, confusing and vulnerable states. These are adult responses to adult issues. We don't need to apologise for having them, to apologise when we feel something in front of another. (I'm so sorry for upsetting *you*, says a bereaved wife to her friend.) If we can feel easier about accepting these as adult emotional responses, we will go a long way to reversing the split between the different parts of ourselves. Childhood can then be reserved for children and for our own histories. As it stands now, we poach the territory of childhood in an attempt to explain ourselves to ourselves, but the act increases rather than heals the splits in our various adult experiences.

Don't Blame the Genes

So Prozac is still being marketed direct to readers of glossy magazines in the US, with the message that deep, dark depression can be turned into sunshine with a daily 20mg dose. Does this wrap things up? Is the happiness now being promised to 17.6 million Americans evidence that biology is king in our psychologies? Should we who practise psychotherapy, psychoanalysis or counselling, give up our couches and take up prescription pads?

To be sure, undoing depression is not easy, and psychological change can often be laboriously slow. God knows, psychotherapists see enough psychological distress to wish that there really were a pill that could do away with human misery. And, undoubtedly, there are many people – in and out of therapy – who find medication extremely helpful.

But the issue raised by this new push by Prozac's manufacturers goes wider than the effectiveness of drug therapy: not so much how medicine, or bio-chemicals, can regularise seratonin levels and thus avert disabling distress, but how distress shapes the bio-chemistry of our bodies; how our neural responses are driven by our psychologies, and how our psychological responses create in us biological signatures that reinforce certain patterns, ways of being and moods.

We're all aware of people whose bodies announce with a shuffle or a bounce how they feel. We are quite accepting of the flu that lays us low psychologically as much as physically. We've even taken on board that our psychologies may have some part to play in susceptibility to illness and recovery from it. But the intriguing question from a psychotherapist's perspective is the way in which an understanding of neuroscience may cast light on psychoanalytic phenomena: for instance, the pressure to re-enact scenarios that are hurtful (the repetition compulsion); the difficulty of confronting psychic pain (repression); and the enormous psychological dissonance that is experienced when one comes out of a depression. The transition from a long-term state of unhappiness to one of contentment is not at all straightforward and can be scary. Contentment may even feel untenable, as though the previously depressed or anxious state had become an unbreakable habit.

Psychotherapists have become rather skilled at hanging in there with patients who are making progress towards change – it can often be excruciating giving up a familiar distress for the discomfort of the new. Getting better, so the old caricature goes, often involves getting worse on the way. It is not simply a question of uncovering and engaging with what has previously been denied. An equally difficult part of psychic change may be adjusting to the unfamiliarity of a new and uninhabited psychological state.

How often have we observed family violence or warring couples without understanding quite what has fuelled the discord? We see moments of tension, and moments of release which look like set pieces. We wonder why the individuals can't quite get themselves off a seemingly mutually destructive track. In my work over the years, I've wondered how apparently hurtful self-inflicted wounds – such as cutting oneself, or impelling oneself to hang over a toilet bowl evacuating food – can provide a physical release. And as more neuropsychological research comes to the fore, I'd wonder too about the way we shape our own individual biology so that psychological distress lays down neural pathways which, if repeated often enough, become like a personal template, inclining our emotions to choose one way rather than another.

It's not that we are driven by our physical responses *per se*, but that our psychological idioms are mirrored in our bodies. We aren't just drama queens in the head: our bodies come to expect the highs and lows of the play we unfold for them. Traumatised Vietnam veterans are a well-documented case in point. These were former combatants whose responses to stress had been so numbed that it took extremely high levels of painful stimulation to trigger off in them the mechanisms we human beings count on to soothe ourselves in moments of extreme difficulty. For one group, it took watching a combat movie for 15 minutes for any significant feelings of pain to be induced. The movie images of horrible violence aroused a state of extreme agitation, which in turn activated their bodies to secrete a natural analgesic equivalent to the sedative impact of 8mg of morphine. In other words, in order to calm themselves they needed *more* rather than less pain; they needed to identify with the extreme violence on screen before their bodies would release a soothing mechanism.

A similar mechanism seems to be at work in a milder form with those old Freudian chestnuts: repetition, repression and the difficulty with resolving neurosis. It's not so much that our bodies crave higher levels of tension as that they seem to favour neural pathways which they have already established.

There are links here between the push to market Prozac as the cure to unhappiness and the debate over whether the different social behaviour of men and women was genetic or cultural in origin. Some might argue that mental pain is biological, some that it's purely in the mind. But the work with the Vietnam vets suggests that we unknowingly coax our neural pathways in particular directions. It follows that an individual confronting the difficulties of psychological change may also be experiencing a sense of discomfort caused by bodily responses that are slightly askew or unfamiliar.

There is another confusion, too. Simply altering a depressed person's biochemistry via medication doesn't necessarily give the individual confidence that their changed mood is their own, to be relied on and stable. Plenty of patients on fluoxetine drugs, of which Prozac is one branded make, are anxious about coming off Prozac because they are unsure whether the change resides in the drug or in themselves.

In the genetics debates, there are many of us who argue that when particular behaviour is encouraged (unconsciously or purposefully) from infancy and is continually reinforced, the behaviour begins to seem completely central to an individual's experience on her or himself. Even though the behaviour is in fact shaped psychologically and culturally, it *feels* fixed and as if it were genetic. Indeed, one way of establishing our uniqueness is to reach for genetics – the real me is my DNA. That seems, at first glance, to seal our distinctiveness and to describe the essence of us. Perhaps, too, it's a way of responding to our perceived powerlessness – to assert that our inviolable core is genetic, an 'I' that stands free of cultural influence.

While such an image is deeply resonant in our culture because it chimes with the old doctrine of predestination, it sidesteps a more complex issue – how far each individual forms him or herself. That such processes are unconscious doesn't make them less profound or influential. We are far more the people we make of ourselves through engaging with our culture than we usually recognise. Our genetics we receive, but we mould aspects of our psychological and our biological signatures in ways that we are only just beginning to understand.

Freudian Slip into Ignorance

B ritish quality newspapers sank to new lows last week in their reporting of a story from a *New York Review of Books* piece by Frederick Crews in November. Crews, a Professor of English and former pro-Freudian literary critic, has renounced Freud and psychoanalysis, and – like the Communist turncoats of the Fifties – he uses everything he can to justify his new position, ridiculing what was once a dearly loved discourse of his.

The *Independent* and (to a lesser extent) the *Observer* then reproduced Crew's arguments. These copied pieces are largely ignorant, and the ignorance they bring to the study of psycho-analysis, and the implicit questioning about the 'talking cure', needs discussing.

Psychoanalysis (in these places) is being discredited on the basis of Freud's alleged manufacturing of his patients' revelations of sexual desire towards the Oedipal parent. Morty Schatzman and now Allen Esterson see no evidence in Freud's accounts that his patients said the things he attributed to them. Rather, they claim, it is Freud who suggested to his patients the idea that they had sexual feelings for their parents. From this, detractors of psychoanalysis (not Schatzman himself) have argued that his theoretical edifice – Oedipus, the Unconscious, Repression – is discredited. Psychoanalysis (the talking cure) and its allied child, psychotherapy, should all come tumbling down.

Undoubtedly, the historical research on Freud is important – not just to correct some of the hagiographical biography which has accompanied the founder of psychoanalysis, but in order to fill out our picture of the origins and development of this important intellectual and clinical discipline. Freud's deeds will continue to be evaluated and re-evaluated. The coming on stream of Freud's personal documents held at the Library of Congress in the year 2000 and on will yield new biographies and new assessments. We can already see publishers brandishing cheque books to scholars who will hit the newly available files. Freud is fascinating and psychoanalysis is fascinating. But the preoccupation with the veracity of his reporting in the present debate raises considerable concern. The Emma Eckstein story is not new. I learned about it as a beginner more than 25 years ago – yet it is recycled now as brand-new, shocking information about Freud's malpractice. The critique of his handling of Dora fills many volumes and has been the subject of countless conferences and seminars. But now uncovering Freud has become synonymous with attacking psychotherapy.

Most disturbing to a present-day practitioner of psychoanalytic psychotherapy is the subtle elision that is employed to
suggest that what Freud practised and understood 100 years ago
is the hallmark of what goes on in the consulting rooms of
today's practitioners, who are practising a craft which is highly
developed and rigorously theorised in both its clinical and tech-
nical applications.

Freud's contribution was enormous. He gave us new ways to
understand dreams; he offered a developmental schema which
understands both human agency and human helplessness; he
proposed a way to understand how the human being psychically manages pain, protects her or himself, how unacceptable
and unallowable ideas find circuitous routes to express themselves, and so on. But psychoanalysis is above all an alive
discipline. It has many different schools of thought and practice
which represent contemporary understandings of Freud's original schema.

Contemporary psychoanalysis and psychotherapy is characterised by a focus on the relationship between analyst and
analysand and the meanings they can make together – meanings that are always provisional, rather than authoritative, about
the events, conflicts and distresses of the analysand's life. Where
nineteenth and early twentieth-century psychoanalysis was
marked by the authority of the doctor, post-war analysis is
marked by a shift in relations between doctor and patient, therapist and client, analyst and analysand, from one of hierarchy to
one of collaboration.

There is no such thing as an expert who interprets. Therapy is
a co-operative effort to create understandings which are of

value. We don't discover in therapy that we conform to Freud's view and wanted to make love with our mother; we grapple for more personal meanings, the sense we have made and are making of our lives. Therapy is a forum for understanding and changing, but not through interpretation being handed down. Therapy is a dialogue between persons, with the focus primarily on the concerns of the one. Where the clinician's agenda takes precedence, we speak of the abuse of therapy or an abusive therapy.

Contemporary psychoanalysis and therapy often centres less on Freud's concern with genital and sexual development than it does on the impediments to trust, to relating, to attachment. While Freud's primal scene is a useful metaphor for some practitioners, it by no means figures as the single, prominent, theoretical linchpin in many others. If we were to look at the history of physics, we would see that many former notions of how the natural world works have now been surpassed, and yet we do not dispute that physics is a way of knowing. We say its ways of knowing are provisional, restricted, useful until superseded. So too with psychoanalysis and psychotherapy. An alive discipline necessarily develops with experience and discards or elaborates previous insights. Some developments (like the challenge to Drive theory, the emergence of Interpersonal theory and Object Relations theory, and Gender awareness) shake its foundations, but yet refashioned in contemporary form, psychoanalysis lives on as a valuable method for making meaning in today's world. We must wonder, then, what is going on here.

The assault is coming from several different places at one time. The American insurance companies, hell-bent on controlling the cost of psychiatric treatments, have been won over by the pharmaceutical companies to the efficacy of 'Managed Care'. Essentially, this means short-term treatment supplemented by Prozac and the various anti-depressants on the market. The allegation of the widespread planting of 'False Memories of Sexual Abuse' by hypnotherapists into the minds of gullible patients joins hands with the current attack. The rolling back of a progressive political agenda, in which a discovery of personal meaning (first engaged with by women in the West in the rap or consciousness group) illuminated other domains, is another. Discussions of masculinity and femininity from a gender-conscious perspective have led to serious questioning about the 'rational' basis of thought and argument. The attack on psychoanalysis, with its stress on the subjective and meaning, is part of the backlash against innovative and timely ways of conceptualising human experience.

While clearing out the cobwebs of psychoanalysis is a noble endeavour, this current assault mischaracterises contemporary practice and is aimed at all derivatives of the 'talking cure'. We would be wise to think before we pounce, and to try to understand the meaning of the attack rather than revel in revelations which are old and not that enlightening.

The Me's I Don't Know

For nearly 100 years, psychoanalysts have employed the concept of repression to explain what happens with emotional scenarios that are unthinkable or indigestible. Originally attached to painful, tragic or sexually inappropriate events, the meaning of repression was soon extended to explain the contents of the unconscious; repressed material became the unrecognised fantasy life of the individual.

Repression is a useful idea in the clinical setting in helping individuals to come to terms with troubling issues just outside their consciousness. When something that has previously been out of view can become visible, there is an inner emotional settling – an 'Aha' not simply of intellectual recognition but of the emotional restoration of a displaced aspect of self.

Psychotherapy and the psychotherapeutic relationship provides the kind of emotional milieu in which it is possible for the individual to recognise the feelings, events and ideas that may cause them to act in ways which conflict with their conscious desires. When previously repressed feelings, memories or emotional tableaux or specific events can be experienced in less threatening circumstances, they can be reintegrated. The person may feel her or himself to be less of a loose cannon, whose unexpected outbursts disrupt the emotional space at any moment. The traumas move back into the past and become part of an understanding of one's development rather than a part of what unexpectedly and unpredictably determines aspects of present life.

Almost everyone accepts the idea of repression now, although in popular culture the word has taken on a specific meaning: 'She's so repressed' suggests that she is emotionally or sexually uptight.

As clinical practice has evolved and moved beyond its original sphere of working with people whose difficulties could be called neuroses to those whose distress cannot be put into such a neat category, psychotherapists have observed how great a disjuncture there can be between people's experience of self and aspects of self that are unknown, split off from them, dissociated.

Today there are many people who seek therapy because they feel an emotional disjuncture: as though parts of themselves are out of reach. Prospective analysands can describe themselves as fragmented and unintegrated even if they are functioning at a very competent level in the world. Other people are aware of living in an emotional deadness; things that should touch them fail to register. Still others discover that their unpredictability is a severe burden to them. They are wary, not knowing which bit of them will pop out next, and they are alarmed by the discord that exists between different parts of themselves.

Many of us are aware of aspects of self that are uneasy with other parts of our self. We don't have a continuing experience of self; rather we have multiple aspects of our personality, some of which sit well with one another, others which cause us some discomfort. We may experience a degree of compartmentalisation, or a sense that different parts of our personality only emerge in particular circumstances.

For many people who seek therapy because they feel unable to integrate positive emotional experiences or build relationships that nourish, the processes of splitting and dissociating may well have colonised aspects of their psychological self. When trying to understand the mechanisms at work in dissociation, I incline towards a mental picture of parts of the self that are in a sense stranded, marooned or in some way separated out from conscious experience. But, unlike repressed material which is located in the unconscious, and which once there is elaborated on and thought about unconsciously, dissociated material is held in a frozen state, detached, parcelled off in its original form.

Some psychotherapists and analysts visualise the psyche as an egg with repression occupying a horizontal cross-section across the upper segment, pressing on the psyche and acting as a constraint. Dissociation, by contrast, is seen to create a vertical barrier down the centre of the egg: a division of the psyche into discrete, separately functioning parts that do not communicate with or know about each other.

Psychotherapists and analysts believe that dissociated material and dissociated parts of self occur because repeated experiences of emotional abuse make it hard for an individual to build up enough emotional strength to assimilate continuing trauma. Many of us will be aware of the phenomenon of cutting off, of dissociating ourselves from unbearable experiences. We may imagine we are not there, that we are looking down on ourselves as in a movie, but that in some essential way we have disengaged or are not deeply involved. It is happening to another part of our self or to someone else.

If painful events cannot afterwards be talked about, listened to in non-threatening circumstances, chewed over, re-lived, they turn into traumas. A trauma doesn't signify a simple event; it is more complex. A trauma ensues when psychologically damaging events are compounded by not being able to be digested. They then have to be set aside, transformed or forgotten in some way in order for the person to carry on.

The recognition of helplessness is one of the most difficult emotional states to assimilate. To accept helplessness, one usually requires the acceptance and validation of another. Without external support, a person can be driven mad by remembering what is denied and negated by others. It is when there is a failure of external support that active, but unconscious, forms of 'forgetting' come in to play. One form is repression, another dissociation. Dissociation occurs when people sustain continual or persistent trauma. Repeated unprocessed emotional injury leads to a part of the person who appears sealed off from and unaffected by the events. The hurtful experiences are zipped up and detached. In this way a functioning part carries on an attenuated life. Encountering these split off, frozen parts of self, in a benign environment enables one to knit together a more substantial experience of self.

Therapy is a Two-Way Process

So we hear once again that it is therapists who are at fault for instigating 'false memories' in those who consult them. Cast in the role of the destroyer of families or the provoker of disputes between children and their parents, irresponsible practitioners with dangerous techniques at their disposal, the therapist has become the new bogey person. But is it true?

Therapy *can* be damaging just like surgery. But it is misleading to suggest, as the press have shouted, that 'recovered memory therapy' is a therapy. What can happen is that, in the course of therapy, people might encounter aspects of their childhood which were previously blocked, unavailable, repressed. When these aspects of experience enter consciousness they are thought about, felt and assimilated in a new way, revising the understanding the person has held of who they are.

What has continued to be remarkable to me in my work is

the way in which an individual can come to therapy, mention that abuse has occurred in childhood, and yet feel unable to work on it. This is not 'recovered' memory, but memory never lost; yet the memory of the events and the effects of the abuse are so painful and damaging that it takes all the person has to mention them. Once mentioned, the person in therapy often wishes to set it aside, to not talk about it, to find an alternative way of explaining their distress. It is often only with great reluctance that the abuse can be talked about at length.

So there is no such thing as recovered memory therapy. If there is a charge to be laid at those whose patients emerge with 'recovered memories', then it should be one of implanting ideas. This has nothing to do with therapy. Therapy involves thinking about the patient/client and his or her experience and together creating understandings of that experience. Therapists who hand down their interpretations as if they were the truth, who tell patients what to think or pronounce on what is really in their heads (or hearts), are caricatures. Such people do exist, as do rotten surgeons, electricians and lawyers, but to think just because one is vulnerable on entering therapy that one is therefore prey to being manipulated is to insult patients and therapists alike – and to misunderstand the nature of therapy and the therapeutic process.

One hugely misunderstood aspect of the psychotherapist's stance has grown around the idea of neutrality. People have taken it to mean that the therapist is a blank screen, doesn't show his or her opinion, doesn't impose his or her feelings on the situation, doesn't feel anything for the patient. These ideas aren't just nonsense, they are impossible. Humans, by their nature, affect one another and – like any relationship – the therapist is affected by the patient and the patient is affected by the therapist. (To return to my earlier point, this means that therapists don't and can't stick ideas into passive patients.)

So therapeutic neutrality is not about not having an opinion or a view, it is far more subtle than that. Therapeutic neutrality is about the psychotherapist's curiosity; it is about being able to approach the individual in therapy with interest and an openness to what they are saying. It's about hearing what is being said and the ways in which it is being told, without preconception.

Therapeutic neutrality means the capacity to observe, to suspend judgement or the rush to explain in favour of sitting with and digesting what she or he is hearing and seeing. It also means being able to tolerate extremely unexpected and strange behaviours explained or performed in the consulting room, so that one can think about them rather than raise a metaphorical eyebrow. Therapeutic neutrality means the psychotherapist is observing any feelings that are aroused by what the patient says or how the patient is, and thinking about those feelings rather than acting on them by flinging them back at the person seeking help.

In the course of their working life, therapists will encounter extremely confusing and often unpleasant phenomena: patients who cut themselves, who pull out their hair as they speak, lie, beat their children, or are violent. Holding a neutral stance towards such phenomena is the *sine qua non* of their beginning to be understood. Therapeutic neutrality provides the base from which the therapist can explore what so troubles the patient. But the therapeutic couple will get nowhere if the stance of the therapist is anything but curious and open. Preconceptions can only get in the way of what might be therapeutic, rendering the patient not the subject of the therapy but rather an object of the therapist's theories.

Of course therapeutic neutrality doesn't nullify knowledge. Knowledge sits beside our interests and provides ways of thinking and conceptualising the patient's difficulties. There is always a creative tension between meeting each patient anew and afresh and seeing their psychic struggles in theoretical terms. What therapeutic neutrality allows the therapist to do is to be genuinely interested in how it is or was for the particular individual, so that their experience can begin to be understood. Nothing could be further from the idea that there is a therapy called recovered memory therapy.

Notes

The Need not to Know
This piece was written in May 1996 at the height of the BSE crisis

Public Emotions and Political Literacy
Antidote can be reached at 5th Floor, 45 Beech Street, London EC2Y 8AD 0171 588 5151

When Truth is not Enough
This article was written in 1995 at the time of the screening of the Channel 4 documentary *Death in the Family*

The Meaning of Money
This article was originally written at the time of the 1996 Budget

Secure Attachments

The Centre for Attachment based psychoanalytic psychotherapy is at 12a Nassington Road, London NW3 0171 433 1263

Smacking II

How to talk so kids will listen and listen so kids will talk by Adele Faber and Elaine Mazlich, Avon Books, New York 1980
Positive Parenting, Elizabeth Hartley-Brewer, Cedar, London 1994

Why Big Boys Don't Cry

The Trouble with Boys by Angela Phillips, Pandora, London 1993

The Other Side of Caring

Between Women: Love, Envy & Competition in Women's Friendships by Luise Eichenbaum and Susie Orbach, Arrow, London 1988

The Political Psyche

The Political Psyche by Andrew Samuels, Routledge, London 1993
The Women's Therapy Centre, 10 Manor Gardens, London N7 6JS 0171 263 6200

Beware the Prejudiced Analyst

Wild Desires and Mistaken Identities by Noreen O'Connor and Joanna Ryan, Virago, London 1993